THE
ESSENCE OF
 FENG
SHUI

Also by Jami Lin

*Jami Lin pioneered the transformation of Feng Shui by integrating
practical interior decorating, and self-development to bring
EarthDesign™ home to the spirit.*

BOOKS

***Feng Shui Today: Earth Design the Added Dimension*—**Deepak
Chopra's review describes this book best...*[Professional interior
designer and Feng Shui expert] "draws from sacred architecture, geo-
mancy, astrology, and the organic approaches of visionary architects.
Jami presents practical and inexpensive ideas to bring harmony to
your surroundings in a book that goes far beyond Feng Shui."*
(EarthDesign, Inc: Literary Division, 1995, ISBN: 0-9643060-9-3.)

***Feng Shui Anthology: Contemporary Earth Design*—**Jami gathered
the industry's most knowledgeable Feng Shui specialists to provide
you with all of their knowledge, along with their practical and easy-
to-follow ideas. Feng Shui Grand Master Lin Yun's words are accu-
rate, *"nothing is left out,"* as *The Anthology* includes Feng Shui
Basics, Feng Shui Schools, Architecture and Landscape, Decorative
Feng Shui, Feng Shui for the Healthy Body, Feng Shui for the
Healthy Home, Feng Shui for the Spirit, and The Divine Plan.
(EarthDesign, Inc: Literary Division, 1997, ISBN: 0-9643060-9-5.)

VIDEO

***Feng Shui Today: Enrich Your Life by Design*—**Fast and fun,
this video, *"heralded as the finest in the industry,"* is jam-packed
with Feng Shui tips through practical, inexpensive, and easy-to-
follow interior decorating ideas. It is produced and directed by
a multi–Emmy Award–winning team. (BC Productions and
EarthDesign, Inc: Literary Division, 1997, ISBN: 0-9643060-6-9.)

MUSIC
Sound Chi: Feng Shui Music to Heal the Home and Spirit, by
Steven Halpern, internationally acclaimed visionary recording artist;
and by Jami Lin.

ESSENTIAL OILS

Feng Shui Essentials™ Jami Lin: Chakra/Bagua Blends™—
The perfect complement to balance your body and your home.
Created with finest quality, 100 percent pure essential oils,
hand-bottled with love based upon the mind-body-spiritual energetics of the Chakras and the Feng Shui/Bagua. (EarthDesign, Inc.,
1-800-EarthDesign.)

SPECIAL PROGRAMS

- Weekend Feng Shui Workshops and five-day
  Intensives—locations throughout the world.
- 4-, 6-, 10-, and 14-hour continuing education programs for Interior Design, Architectural, and Real
  Estate professionals.
- Inspirational, motivational, and highly informative
  talks, lectures, seminars, and workshops at design and
  architecture, real estate, landscape, builder, and
  spiritual organizations.
- Custom lectures, workshops, and intensives available upon request.

FENG SHUI CONSULTATIONS

Personalized Feng Shui on-site or phone consultations for residential,
corporate, health-care, retail, hospitality facilities, and developers.
Consultations are available for all stages of Feng Shui design: predevelopment and site consideration through existing structures.

FENG SHUI INTERIOR DESIGN

From predevelopment and space planning to architectural detailing, fin-
ishes, furnishings, and accessories, Jami Lin and her staff of professional
interior designers will co-create your complete Feng Shui environment.
Residential, corporate, health-care, retail, and hospitality facilities.

For information, contact:
EarthDesign Inc.,™ P.O. Box 530725, Miami Shores, FL 33153
(305) 756-6426

Please visit Jami Lin's EarthDesign Website at:
www.gate.net/~earthdes

THE ESSENCE OF FENG SHUI

Balancing Your Body, Home, and Life with Fragrance

JAMI LIN

Hay House, Inc.
Carlsbad, CA

Published and distributed in the United States by:
Hay House, Inc., P.O. Box 5100, Carlsbad, CA 92018-5100
(800) 654-5126 • (800) 650-5115 (fax)

Edited by: Jill Kramer • Designed by: Jenny Richards
Interior Artwork: Paul Kane, Ardis Heiman, and Jami Lin

The author of this book does not dispense medical advice or prescribe the use of any technique as a form of treatment for physical or medical problems without the advice of a physician, either directly or indirectly. The intent of the author is only to offer information of a general nature to help you in your quest for emotional and spiritual well-being. In the event you use any of the information in this book for yourself, which is your constitutional right, the author and the publisher assume no responsibility for your actions.

Library of Congress Cataloging-in-Publication Data

Lin, Jami.
      The essence of Feng Shui : balancing your body, home, and life
with fragrance / Jami Lin.
         p.   cm.
     ISBN 1-56170-567-5 (pbk.)
     1. Feng-shui.   2. Essences and essential oils—Miscellanea.
3. Odors—Miscellanea.   I. Title.
BF1779.F4L5715   1998
133.3'337—dc21   98-17035
                                           CIP

ISBN 1-56170-567-5

01 00 99 98   4 3 2 1
First Printing, September 1998

Printed in the United States of America

*Smell is the potent wizard that
transports us across thousands of miles
and all the years we have lived.*

— Helen Keller

*Furniture gleaming with the patina
of time itself in the room we would share;
the rarest flowers, mingling aromas
with amber's uncertain redolence;
encrusted ceilings echoed in the mirrors
and Eastern splendor on the walls—
here all would whisper to the soul in secret....*

— Baudelaire
(Translated by Richard Howard)

Contents

- Earth Design Is the Root
- Fragrance Is the Catalyst
- Dedication Is the Key
- Unlimited Potential
- The Power of Chi
- Symbols and Personal Chi
- Sacred Geometry

- Smells: Past, Present, and Future
- The Essence of Feng Shui
- Setting Goals—Let's Do It!
- Awareness of Thought
- Essential Oils—The Origins of Good Scents
- Fragrant Chi
- Body
- Mind
- Spirit
- The Three Levels of Human Beings
- The Symbolism of the Plant

- The Birth of the Tree of Life
- The Grand Design
- The Seed of Life
- The Vessels
- Taking Root

Foreword by
FENG SHUI GRAND MASTER LIN YUN*

Jami Lin (right) with Lin Yun

There are many books being published, but only a scarce few impact on the intellect. Regardless of one's degree of understanding (or endorsement), *The Essence of Feng Shui,* the latest work by my good friend Jami Lin, allows one to freely explore and discover one's "inner truth." Jami's book actually has, as a matter of universal event, awakened the subdued intellect with sparkling and wonderful exponential ripples. By thoroughly studying *The Essence of Feng Shui,* one develops a more profound understanding of, and appreciation for, life, thereby allowing one to experience life's ultimate possibilities and joys.

From a certain perspective, books that offer valuable guidance fall under one of two main categories: those which propagate mundane knowledge and those which explain transcendental knowledge. Each is unique in strengths and emphasis. *The Essence of Feng Shui,* however, is not only a masterpiece that brings a new dimension to the world of publishing, it is a book that spans both the mundane and the transcendental. In reading *The Essence of Feng Shui,* one realizes that Jami is clearly and precisely focused on how fragrance and scent bring harmony to one's body, family, society, and life. On this point, Jami's methods coincide with methods that I have developed in the fourth and current stage of Black Sect Tantric Buddhism, including my theories and practice on how to work with scent and the sense of smell, chi cultivation, Feng Shui adjustments, and the application of minor transcendental adjustments to enhance, revitalize, or rectify one's living condition. Furthermore, Jami's studies and analyses are far more lucid and comprehensible than mine. In fact, a thorough understanding of this wonderful book allows Feng Shui students, experts, and scholars alike to deduce this important revelation: In addition to understanding and appreciating life through the five senses, one could fine-tune one's life by working with fragrance, be it body scents or others, to influence the health, security, happiness, psychological balance, and harmony of one's family and society.

The Essence of Feng Shui is a book that is at once rooted in tradition, and going beyond. It begins with a discussion on the quintessence of Feng Shui and touches on the interplay between the earth's root, chi, and scent, along with the physiological, psychological, and spiritual well-being of mankind. Jami proceeds to share insights on the body's energy centers by analyzing the various chakras. Having explained the use of the eight trigrams in pinpointing the energy centers in one's environment, she shares various ways of assessing one's life situation. In expounding the application of transcendental and mundane solutions to adjust one's living conditions, Jami emphasizes the use of fragrance, both as a stand-alone solution and as an enhancement to other solutions. Working with yin-yang theory, logic, and chi, Jami's methods correspond to the I Ching's "permanent ways" and coincide with the methods of the Black Sect Tantric Buddhist school of Feng Shui, which applies visible forms (yang), invisible elements (yin), and exterior and interior factors in accordance with principles of science and spiritual studies.

For all these reasons, this book is invaluable to me. Accordingly, due to my personal belief that happiness is multiplied through sharing, I highly recommend *The Essence of Feng Shui* as a way to share the ultimate pleasure of scent to inspire seekers to attain knowledge, fortune, pure heart, and good karma. In this way, they too can take part in a journey of realization into the universe of the miraculous, mystical, and invaluable effects—not only of scents, spices, and fragrances, but also of the application of such through spraying, rubbing, smearing, sprinkling, and "spritzing."

*(Translated by Jonathan W. Y. Chau)

xiv

Acknowledgments

A special thanks to my family: I love you.
Joel Alan Levy
Ardis Heiman
Mitzi and Eddy Levy

I couldn't have done it without you. Thank you.
Maggie Leyes
Elizabeth Pierra-Quintana
Paul Kane
Ellen Whitehurst

Thanks for your special help.
Kurt Ludwig Nubling and Ute Leube of Primavera Life:
(fine essential oils!)

Art and Susan Rochlin, Heidi Reeve, Rita Lewison-Singer,
Jane Hayden, Carol Corio, Lisa Roggow, Steve Greenberg, Joel Kaplan,
Denny Fairchild, Robert Welsh, Lori Hodges, Roberta Scimone,
Ryan Aulton, Lance Stelzer, Dan Liss, Kathy Tumson, Mike Osterley,
Louise Hay, Reid Tracy, Jill Kramer, and Jenny Richards

I wish to honor my Feng Shui teachers and colleagues—my
friends—whose individual support and love continue to inspire
me through their dedication to share this wonderful gift.

My teachers:
Masters: Lin Yun, Lillian Too, Jes T. Y. Lim, and Derek Walters

Juan and Carmen Alvarez, Mary Buckley, Carol Bridges, Crystal Chu,
Terah Kathryn Collins, Jeanne D'Brant, Sheree J. Deneen, Mary Dennis,
Dennis Fairchild, Andrew and Sally Fretwell, Shera Gabriel,
Lillian Lesefko Garnier, Hope Karan Gerecht, Roger Green, Johndennis
Kaiten Govert, Helen and James Jay, Linda M. Johnson, Mark Johnson,
Katrine T. Karley, David Daniel Kennedy, Kirsten Lagatree, Pamela Laurence,

Toni Lefler, Melanie Lewandowski, Maggie Leyes, Denise Linn,
Bob and Celeste Longacre, Ho Lynn, A. T. Mann, Kathy Mann,
James Allyn Moser, Cynthia Murray, Elaine Paris, Richard L. Phillips,
Hank Reisen, Sarah Rossbach, Susan H. Ruzickza, Nancy SantoPietro,
Shelley Sparks, William Spear, Angel Thompson, Pamela Tollefson,
Derek Walters, Angi Ma Wong, Seann Xenja, and Kathy Zimmerman

...and to all my "helpful people" whom
I may not ever have the good fortune
to meet, I thank and appreciate
you the most.....

Introduction

Feng Shui (pronounced *FUNG-SHWAY*) has been my greatest blessing—all aspects of my life have grown. In my dedication to share Feng Shui with others, I have met many interesting and wonderful people whose quest, like mine, is to explore personal human potential more deeply. Fragrant Feng Shui is the search for the fragrant fullness of life experience: What does life feel, taste, and smell like while on the path of unlimited possibility?

Back to my college vision (for those who have read my previous introductions), the more I explore my spiritual path, the more excited I get about the universal interpretations of Nature's workings and how it personally applies to each one of us. And as a Gemini messenger, I can't help immersing myself in it—I have released four Feng Shui publications in as many years. I have exhaustively learned that it is more productive to control my excitement about life's inner mysteries at the grocery checkout line and to channel that energy into writing with the intent of sharing my enthusiasm with you. I have found that my communication is a function of my desire to explore my own path, while at the same time share a universally fragrant inner journey that everyone can partake in.

Feng Shui consistently teaches me to work within the flow to be happy. The more fulfilled and happier you are, my dear reader, the happier everybody else is! But why fragrance? Observing the body- and home-fragrance industries, I have found that pleasant smells make people feel good.

Fragrance makes me happy. I love experimenting with essential oils on my body and in my home. So, the essence of this book is to incorporate fragrance into your life to make you feel good. The technique may be as simple as spraying your body and home with your selected fragrance. (I welcome you to go right to chapter 7 for an immediate smell-good fix.)

However, in following the scent for my personal happiness, I discovered that fragrance can also be a delicious and purposeful tool for personal expansion. It is tied to interpretations of the cosmos that were presented to us through the ages by worldwide Earth peoples. We are graced to receive their most sacred universal teachings, which include the integration of ceremonial fragrance to maximize spiritual growth and individual potential.

While all traditions bring us valuable wisdom, my foremost intention in all the work that I do is to encourage you to seek truth in accordance with your own belief system. Guided by your own development, the more you tap into your spiritual source, the collective unconscious, God, Great Spirit, Nature, Mother Goddess, Jesus, the Divine Universe—or whatever sacred definition works for you—the more you will find the answers according to your own truth.

In the same way that Feng Shui and its manifestation is based upon interpretation of certain basic concepts, practitioner experience and intuition, the client's Chi, and most important, doing the work with intention, spiritual evolution asks that you do the same. Through your examination of Feng Shui, you'll see that it can be a great vehicle to open up spiritual pathways, while at the same time helping you live in its beauty, harmony, and grace.

My greatest desire is that you experience life with the utmost joy. This is how, collectively, we can transform the planet into the Age of Aquarius, the Age of Light, the New Millennium, and the prophetic splendor of the many Earth traditions. So my goal, whatever your path may be, is to welcome you to search for your own truth, questioning tradition as well as my interpretations (since you may find them different from yours), so that you may live in the richness of your own path. This is the catalyst in making your Feng Shui experience most effective.

Part I of this book explores wisdom from many traditions, defining Nature's mysteries and its relationship to human beings. Such "sage-old" traditions as Chinese, Hindu, and Kabbalistic teachings are connected through their universal understanding of energy, sacred geometry, and symbolism. This wisdom will help you understand how to use essential oils to enhance the specific body (Chakra) and home (Bagua) energy centers.

Continuing with your exploration and mine, this ancient knowledge validates that spiritual development is not about external things; it is about inner growth, or developing personal Chi (life energy).

With the understanding of how and why the body and home energy centers are connected, Part II explains how we can look inward to ask questions about our life's desires. Specific fragrances, scientifically and symbolically linked to each of the home/body energy centers, are discussed, along with how to use them. You can then easily determine which oils to use to enhance all aspects of your life. I have stated that "if it catches your eye, it alters Chi," so it is only natural that "if it catches your nose, it also alters Chi," which is clearly the next dimension of Earth Design.

In Fragrant Feng Shui, fragrance amplifies the development of our personal Chi by linking the energy centers of the home and body with the healing and life-enhancing qualities of specific oils. Our elders combined fragrance in their rituals to magnify their inner quests; why shouldn't we do the same in our homes and bodies? Through simple Fragrant Feng Shui adjustments, changes, and ceremonies, you can add fragrance to clear and energize the energy centers of *your* home and body. You can also *code* your furniture and accessories, symbolically located in significant energy centers, to manifest your Feng Shui results.

While I could have easily combined home and body together with Feng Shui fragrance, I am grateful that all the ancient tools are available so we can fully explore a myriad of possibilities. I am appreciative of your indulgence with my search, my need to share, my desire to incorporate fragrance in my Feng Shui experience, and most important, the fact that you provide me with an outlet, so as not to freak everybody out at the grocery store.

With loving good scents,

Jami Lin
Fall 1998

PART I

The Foundation of Fragrant Feng Shui

Good Scents

Neat:

Direct or straight application for cuts, bruises, and pimples should only be used with non-irritant oils such as lavender, sandalwood, and ylang ylang. Always do a very small patch test, and keep oils away from the eyes.

Inhalation:

Use 1–3 drops in a bowl of hot water, put towel over head, inhale or use micro diffuser, inhale until you stop smelling oil, 15–20 minutes; repeat every 3–4 hours.

Compresses:

Hot compresses are great for relieving pain and inflammation. In a bowl with very hot water, add 5 drops of oil. Dip face cloth in, squeeze out water, and place on body.

Cold compresses (using cold water in above instructions) are good for reducing swelling, for sprains, and for headaches.

Topical Use:

Use 50–60 drops to a bottle of 30 ml (1 oz.) carrier oil.

Humidifiers:

Great for winters with dry heaters! Add 3–10 drops to the water, and repeat after a few hours.

Caution: *Throughout the text, oils in italics should never be used during pregnancy.*

Applications

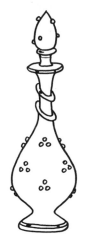

CHAPTER 1

The Essence of Feng Shui

Feng Shui, the Chinese art of placement, is "essentially" about consciously redesigning any environment according to ancient concepts, with specific goals and intentions. The basics can be as simple as moving existing furniture and accessories around your home or office to make positive changes in your life—with the added benefit of surrounding yourself in beauty.

**What a concept—
decorating for greater health, wealth, and happiness!**

Why incorporate fragrance? *The Essence of Feng Shui* is good scents Feng Shui. And...

because they smell good—another profound concept!

Using fragrances in your life can assist you in accomplishing your goals more deliciously, and when combined with your Feng Shui experience, ooh-la-la. The purpose of learning more about fragrance and how it is linked to Feng Shui is to optimize the changes you want to make so that you are able to reach your goals faster and start creating a better life NOW!

Fragrance use as part of the Feng Shui experience can be as simple as purchasing a small vial of essential oil and making a spritzer bottle full of great-smelling home spray. You can begin today, right now, and it is easier than you think. Start with the "grand dame" of essential oils: lavender. It is one of the most versatile essential oils, with many great therapeutic qualities, as well as a balancing effect—and its fragrance is pleasing to almost everyone. Essential oils, which are super-concentrated pure fragrances, are usually packaged in ounce-sized bottles and can be purchased at any health food store. To make a spray for your home, add between 18 and 36 drops of essential oil to a two-ounce, dark glass spray bottle (plastic and light alter the oils), and fill the rest with pure or distilled water. Shake the bottle to mix the ingredients, and you are set to start spraying.

This method makes the essential oils accessible at any time; a small bottle can even be slipped in a purse or briefcase to use at the office or in the car. It is also a very inexpensive Feng Shui cure. For just pennies, you can make up a spritzer bottle of Feng Shui fragrance. Since most vials of pure essential oil can be purchased for under $20, and many under $10, it is one of the most inexpensive Feng Shui adjustments you can make.

The potential is limitless, easily available/accessible, and the dent in your wallet is minimal.

When you go to the store to experiment with the smells that you would like to begin using, consider the following oils. You may also want to pick up a decorative basket to *house* your collection (I have a wicker one with a handle so it is easy to carry).

Here are your Fragrant Feng Shui starter oils:

atlas cedarwood, basil, bergamot, *black pepper,*
roman chamomile, *cinnamon, clary sage, clove,*
cypress, eucalyptus, frankincense, geranium,
ginger, grapefruit, jasmine, *juniper,* lavender,
lemon, orange, patchouli, *peppermint,* pine, rose,
rosemary, sandalwood, *thyme,* vetiver, ylang ylang

Caution: *Essential oils in italics should never be used during pregnancy.*

Essential oils should never be drunk or used for any purpose other than that for which they are intended. Most must never be applied directly to the skin, but mixed with either purified water or a carrier oil. If you have any questions or concerns, please seek the advice of a professional aromatherapist.

Then, let your nose always be your guide!

If it smells good to you, it will be good for you and your Feng Shui experience. We will explore more of the whys and wherefores, but for now, trust your nose and start making your Fragrant Feng Shui sprays.

Earth Design Is the Root

Throughout the ages, people have closely observed Nature's workings and symbols. They intuitively incorporated these natural laws and symbols into their homes, sacred spaces, and lives. This art of bringing Nature's perfection into a space to bring balance and harmony is Earth Design, or Universal Feng Shui; it is an art that has evolved from many traditions all over the world. While we will explore Feng Shui and its symbolic tool, the Bagua, in more depth later, I invite you to read the fascinating background and techniques of Earth Design from many different traditions and cultures.[1]

Feng Shui is about making changes in your environment that will support positive changes in your life. It is about altering your space and your life by moving furniture and accessories, using colors and textures, as well as incorporating fragrance. And while this is a noble pursuit, if there is no intent behind the Feng Shui changes you make, it will not be effective.

The primary rule of Feng Shui: Know your intentions!

When you answer the question, "What life change do I want to accomplish with this Feng Shui adjustment?" then you can determine what accessory to move, where to put it, and what fragrance to use to

---

[1] Of course I recommend my first book, *Feng Shui Today: Earth Design the Added Dimension* for a complete look at the history and the whys and wherefores of Feng Shui and Earth Design, and *The Feng Shui Anthology*.

make the Feng Shui connection.

Feng Shui is about enhancing your environment, the places where you live and work.[2] These are the places where you spend a great deal of your time. Home is the vessel in which you live, but what is your *primary* vessel? Many of the traditions that we will be exploring understood that your body is the vessel that your soul energy or essence is poured into. Since your body is the primary vessel where you spend all your time, why not learn how to use fragrance in your Feng Shui experience to enhance your body, as well as your home and life? Fragrant Feng Shui is about getting your body involved!

Essentially, let's get your body into Feng Shui action!

I was getting prepared to write this book, but with all the traveling, classes, and consultations I had been doing, I hadn't had time to clear my head. The best way to clean the cobwebs out of your life (and head!) is to do a thorough Feng Shui "spring cleaning"—give away everything that you do not love, find beautiful, or haven't used in the past two years (two years is actually conservative—I'd like to say six months!). With this in mind, I knew that my walk-in closet was the target.

I had no thoughts of any physical manifestation that I wanted from this Feng Shui adjustment, just a wondrous closet and a head free and clean. So with my slogan "No mercy" in mind, I began the attack on the closet. As I was working, my nose began to run. "Oh no," I said to myself, "the ol' snort and blow!" Suffering through, I filled three yard-size garbage bags to be given to charity.

You would think that once the dust settled from my closet purge, my nose would equalize, but it just wouldn't. I felt myself on the verge of a good head cold. Then it hit me: During each previous mega-cleaning episode, my nose had always started to run and had grown into a cold. So when I finished, I got out the eucalyptus oil and mixed it with a carrier oil (jojoba), and rubbed it on my chest. Aahhh! (Grandma was right when she used Vicks Vapo-Rub with its eucalyptus smell; this oil has great healing properties for the lungs and respiratory system.) I also put a drop of it on my nightgown and went to sleep to regenerate and nurture.

---

[2] In Fragrant Feng Shui, I speak globally of your space as your home, as it is your heart center, and the main energetic environment where you spend the most time. However, the same concepts apply to any other space you inhabit: office, boat, vacation condo, store, health-care facility, restaurant, and so on.

While I was resting, I realized that cleaning my closet had always been much more than a release of unnecessary clutter. It was literally a cleansing of physical toxins from my body and metaphorically a clearing of my mind to allow new wonders to present themselves. Both closet and mind were cleansed in the process.

If you really want to make a difference in your life with Fragrant Feng Shui, go clean your closet. Open the way for new body, mind, and spiritual experiences; open to all possibilities.

This is Feng Shui good scents! Ready?

Fragrance Is the Catalyst

As with Feng Shui, the art of using essential oil fragrances stems from ancient traditions and perhaps a little mystery. The alchemy of fragrance is truly the union of science and magic—it enhances the positive life changes Feng Shui can create in your life.

Since recorded time, fragrance has been used in homes and sacred spaces to shift energy and create a more balanced environment. It has also been used as an ointment for the body to bless it and raise consciousness. Many traditions throughout history used fragrance on their bodies and in their temples, so why shouldn't we?

Let's look at how the magic of essence works:

While working on my last book, The Feng Shui Anthology, *there were two authors whom I had contacted to contribute an article. With my deadline closing in and having had no confirmation from them, I went into the Helpful People area[3] of my home and office. I gave them a good spritz of my essential oil blend formulated for this area—a mix of lavender,* peppermint,* *and lemon. These oils have special properties that facilitate communication, relaxation, clarity of thought, and acceptance. These were all qualities I needed as the stress mounted and I was unsure of the final outcome of my book. As I sprayed, I focused on my intention that all who contributed to the book would benefit from it as well as enhance the project. Within a week, out of*

---

[3] We will learn more about specific areas of the home and how to incorporate fragrance in chapter 5.

5

nowhere, both authors called and committed to deadlines.

This Feng Shui adjustment that I did in my home and office cer-tainly helped me with my goal of giving my readers the best possible book. It also had an effect on my body. The fragrance helped me release all the tension I had bottled inside due to my deadline and the articles that were missing. When I let go of that stress and clogged-up energy, I allowed room for the Universe to manifest its energy—the articles! This is the essence and magic of Feng Shui! Do you have a tense or stressful situation in your life at this moment? Use your lavender spray; start spraying and de-stressing.

Caution: Peppermint *should never be used during pregnancy.*

How do we get our body involved in Feng Shui? Let's work some fragrant magic!

But, it is truly *your* alchemy—your commitment, faith, and convic-tion to making desirable changes in your life—that works its transfor-mative powers when using fragrance to increase harmony in your life. The prerequisite for Fragrant Feng Shui, like traditional Feng Shui, is that you first know how you want to change and how you want to enhance your life. Then you can begin to move toward those changes.

Dedication Is the Key

No amount of spraying fragrance in the air can change a bad situa-tion by itself. Commitment to change also calls for dedication. The art of magic (not illusionists!) is really the concentrated use of personal power to achieve your results, after learning and practicing how to use focus and intent.

And I guess I know a bit about magic myself. I have been having great fun incorporating Feng Shui into my life and have gotten pretty good at creating positive results. In fact, after the episode with the two authors and the anthology, my editor began to call me the Magic Princess. While there are never any guarantees, it seems that often all I have to do is consciously ask and some kind of magic will happen. But I'm dedicated, too.

Dedication is important. Even with the magic of Feng Shui (and magic there is!) you still have to go out and make the effort. You won't get a better job or find your perfect life-mate unless you go looking for one. That doesn't mean, however, that you can't give Mother Nature a push. Why not learn to use all the tools possible to create a richer life experience?

Need to get motivated? Make a spray of one of these oils to help get you started:

bergamot	cypress	pine
black pepper	grapefruit	*peppermint*
clove	lemon	*rosemary*

Unlimited Potential

It makes perfect "scents" not only to make positive changes in your life, but to explore all the possibilities that life has to offer. Fragrant Feng Shui links your body and environment to your desired intention and individual potential.

In exploring your own potential, it is vital to develop and nurture your personal energy. This means recognizing nonproductive life issues that grab on to your life energy and hold you back from becoming all that you can be. If your personal energy (your thoughts and actions) is caught up in old, unresolved issues, then there isn't enough left to apply to your potential. Until you free up this energy, you cannot create your greatest future.

Personal potential oils—for more fulfilling life experiences, try using these:

benzoin	geranium	roman chamomile
clary sage	jasmine	rose
	lavender	ylang ylang

Caution: *Throughout the text, oils in italics should never be used during pregnancy.*

An issue:

As a little girl, I grew up having all my needs met. I enjoyed sleep-away camp and birthdays that never lacked for great presents. In college, the illusion dissolved with my generous stepfather's passing; he had major unresolved financial problems. And watching the wolf at Mom's door, I vowed that I would never allow myself to get into that position. My unresolved issues included financial security, fear, holding on to my personal power/independence, and control of my own future.

Resolution preview:

Through Fragrant Feng Shui, I addressed the issues using the Career Area of the Bagua/Root Chakra and the Wealth Area/Will Chakra.[4]

Recognition:

I realized that if I could lighten up about my bag-lady issues, my journey through life would be more calm, gracious, and devoid of intense paranoia. I would also free up energy to explore opportunities for career and financial growth, which is easier to recognize without my do-it-to-myself stress. And, life would be more fun!

If you spend time focusing on yourself, you can identify the illusion of your issues and your limiting baggage (like my life-restricting fear of becoming a bag lady). Fragrant Feng Shui can then help you mitigate and possibly resolve them.

Awareness of your issues amplifies the magical outcome in your Feng Shui experience. And while you work on yourself, Feng Shui-ing your environment, you are not only freeing up energy from old baggage, you are strengthening personal Chi, your life energy.

There are even liberating oils to help you "let go." Try:

bergamot	grapefruit	mandarin
coriander	lime	neroli
	lavender	rose

---

[4] As explained in chapter 4, Chakras are energy centers in your body, and the Bagua (see chapter 5) defines energy centers within a space. Working with these energy centers leads to positive life changes.

8

The Power of Chi

In Feng Shui there is a substance that is the key. It is the breath of all life—it is your *breath*. This universal life force is known as the *spirit* or *soul*. And as a rose by any other name would smell as sweet, it is known as *Pneuma* to the Greeks, *Prana* to the Hindus, *Ruah* to the Hebrews, *Ki* to the Japanese, and *Chi* to the Chinese.

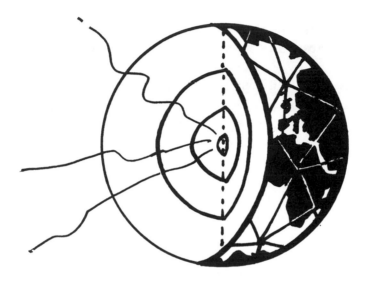

Balanced Chi moves in a smooth, curvilinear pattern. As it moves through the earth, it forms undulating lines that circle the globe. As it reaches the surface, it spirals up and out to nurture the ground and everything that lives on it, from plants to human beings.

The life force of Chi is the glue that holds everything together.

Chi is:

- the vitality of your body.
- soul-sustaining nutrients that come from Heaven.
- life-sustaining nutrients that come from Earth.

Chi is also:

- the momentum of such natural cycles as the seasons, along with birth, death, and rebirth.

- the space between submolecular particles (which we will use for Fragrant Feng Shui coding).
- the space between the notes in music.
- the rush of goose bumps and sensual arousal.
- intuition in man and instinct in animals.
- the heat of the sun and the whoosh of an ocean surge.
- light dancing through a prism.

Chi represents your thoughts and visions for the creation of a perpetually fulfilling life.

In a positive Feng Shui environment, Chi flows not too fast, not too slow, but in perfect harmony through your environment and your life. It nurtures every space as it passes through, in the same way that each breath you take nurtures every cell and fiber of your body. If Chi is not flowing harmoniously, your life will be out of balance, and problems will begin to manifest. Feng Shui is about solutions to this problem. By making changes to your decor, you create beneficial energy shifts, which in turn make subtle, positive life shifts.

Symbols and Personal Chi

In your mind's eye, visualize yourself as a seedling, growing into the green freshness of childhood and learning about stability as your root system develops; then as you mature, you are able to blossom into the fullness of your potential. Many traditions stemming from both the Kabbalists and the Native Americans have used the tree as just such a symbol, one that represents the process of developing personal Chi and of growing into a better person. What a wonderful symbol, a Tree of Life! A tree, like all other plants, needs Heaven and Earth Chi to grow, the same way you do. And guess what?

All the fragrances that we are going to use come from plants! Plant Chi! Tree Chi Oil!

Tea tree oil...or tree chi oil!? I couldn't resist the wonderful play on words! Tea tree oil has many uses. As an immuno-stimulant, it is effective against infectious organisms such as bacteria, fungi, and viruses. When you are doing your Feng Shui spring cleaning, put it in your warm washing water as a great natural disinfectant. It is also a wonderful skin care oil and is used in many naturally made soaps, toothpastes, and deodorants.

Symbols are very important in Feng Shui. The things that you choose to decorate your home and office with are symbolic of what you would like to accomplish. Feng Shui is not about following outdated rules or choosing some other culture's symbols. It is about creating your own symbols based on your inner knowledge, combined with ancient wisdom. These symbols will then gain personal meaning and help you grow your own tree of life, full of abundant personal Chi.

The essential oils that you will be using have symbolic representations as well. As you grow more familiar with their physical, psychological, and spiritual healing qualities, you will be able to use them in a very personal way. The suggestions for their application are merely a starting point that should light the spark for your own imaginative uses.

Feng Shui is about using symbols to cultivate personal energy.

Sacred Geometry

The use of symbols invariably leads us to sacred geometry. Since ancient times, elders have passed down their knowledge through symbols such as spirals, pyramid shapes, the tree of life, circles—wholeness of the universe—and yin-yang arranged by the laws of nature. Everything in the universe is arranged according to sets of invisible mathematical rules that govern the structure and proportions of everything from the rotation of the planets to the curve of a cathedral arch. This body of knowledge that governs our universe is called sacred geometry.

Geometry literally means "the measurement of earth or land." It is a branch of mathematics that deals with the properties and relations of magnitude. Sacred geometry uses these mathematical symbols to define the workings of the earth and the cosmos. From studying it, you can learn about how the microcosm, or life on a small scale, mirrors the macrocosm, or life on the large scale. The same spiral pattern on a seashell (microcosm) is seen in the swirling mass of a distant galaxy (macrocosm).

Sacred geometry also governs the evolution of human beings. The ancients, being attuned to the heartbeat of Nature, intuited these rules. From this knowledge they were able to set up systems of symbols that explained their very existence on Earth! In Fragrant Feng Shui, you will be exploring a number of these systems, including the Kabbalistic Tree of Life, the Indian Chakra system, and the Feng Shui Bagua. Through symbolism, they define the energy centers in your body, home, and life.

Once you know where the energy centers are and have learned to cultivate your own personal energy, you can begin to create the kind of life you have always dreamed of. But you should not blindly follow another's system. By learning what those who came before you knew, you can set up a solid foundation of *self-understanding* and how you can change by cultivating your personal Chi. From there you can learn to use your own personal system that incorporates the important link of essential oil fragrances.

Feng Shui has evolved throughout history and continues to do so. Even though I am going to present traditional and spiritual references that are universal in scope to explain why and how to incorporate fragrance in your Feng Shui experience, it is certainly not necessary that you adopt any of these traditions in your religious or spiritual life. In fact, I encourage you to use this information as a starting point for making your own Feng Shui symbols and rituals.

As "encouragement," a good oil to help you culti-vate and grow your personal Chi is roman chamomile.

Fragrant Feng Shui has its roots in universal Chi energy, ancient traditions, sacred geometry, symbolism, and the development of personal Chi. It will teach you to explore how each of these factors plays out in your day-to-day life so that you can begin tapping into your untold potential as you spiral into more good scents.

Good Scents

Massage Oil:

Combine the essential oil you are "in the mood for" during this most special experience.

10–30 drops	30 ml (1 oz.) carrier
18–24 drops	60 ml carrier
36–48 drops	120 ml carrier

Bath:

Blend 5–15 drops in 2 tbs. of honey, and add to tub of warm water; soak for 20 minutes.

Jacuzzi:

Add 3 drops for each person; repeat every 10–15 minutes.

Sauna:

Dilute 1–2 drops of eucalyptus, tea tree, and pine and throw it on the heat source.

Bath Salts:

Use 5–8 drops of oil per cup of Epsom salts (magnesium sulfate), sea salts, and/or baking soda, and dissolve in tub. My favorite! Salts pull toxins out of your body while you soak. Ahh!

Salt Glow:

Rub bath salt mixture on clean, wet skin to detoxify and stimulate healthy skin.

Douche:

Combine 10–40 drops per pint warm water, and shake.

Caution: *Throughout the text, oils in italics should never be used during pregnancy.*

Applications

CHAPTER 2

The
Essence
of Fragrance

Your life is linked from moment to moment by scents—from the perfume or cologne that you put on after your shower, to the coffee brewing in the kitchen, to the fresh breeze as you reach outside for the morning paper. The smells that make up your day are not always pleasant, however. A blast of exhaust fumes and garbage left too long in the can are sharp reminders of the more unseemly side of life. But it is this wide range of smells that helps create the intricate and detailed fabric of daily life.

Every smell, whether you are conscious of it or not, creates an experience of the senses. Even the thought of exhaust fumes immediately sends us mental images of being stuck in rush-hour traffic, the hot sun beating through the window, and an old dump truck spewing forth thick clouds of black smoke. Conversely, a pleasurable fragrance, such as a whiff of perfume, might send you back to your warm, steamy bath and soft towel from the morning.

Smells fill your day to such an extent that you may often fail to realize the variety of sensory input that you get through your nose. When you pay attention to the mental effect a smell creates, it is easy to see how a whole visual scenario is painted in your mind's eye.

Fragrance is always present, and you are always affected.
It fills your day in the same way it fills your space.

A whiff of lilacs may send you back to your great-aunt's garden, allowing you to recall those sunny Sunday afternoons when the family gathered for iced tea. The smell of chalk may place you in a grade-school classroom complete with your fifth-grade teacher and the class bully sitting at the desk beside you. And what about the smell of pine? Your mind may go racing back to a walk in the woods with snow falling gently on your coat, or picking out a Christmas tree with your father.

> *The summer between high school and college, I had the great fortune of working in Yellowstone National Park. I was taken by its beauty and grandeur, so unlike the landscape I had grown up with. The park is a thermal "hot spot" and is well known for its geysers. I was enthralled with these holes that swirled with beautiful colors and then sprayed their hot, sulphur-scented water into the air. The wind would carry the mist from the flow, and I would relish being caught in its subtle shower. (Not unlike the feeling of spraying myself with an essential oil spray!) By the time it reached me, the drops were light, cool, and scented with the smell of sulphur. I loved it!*

My story illustrates just how subjective smell is. To most people, sulphur has a negative connotation linked to rotten eggs (and the devil!). But to me, the smell of sulphur (having never smelled a rotten egg) had no negative association. It is linked only to wonderful memories of a magical place and an important time of transition in my life.

Exercise:

Try this simple exercise with smell to become familiar with how potent its power really is. Read the list of smells that follow and write down what images first come to your mind. What is the experience like? Pleasant? Frightening? Sad? Joyful? Painful? Melancholy? How old are you? What are you wearing? Who else emerges in the picture that you have associated with the smell?

- oranges
- candles that have just been blown out
- freshly baked peanut butter cookies
- a wet wool sweater
- bread baking in the oven
- fingerpaint

- gasoline
- ammonia
- permanent magic markers
- a freshly bathed baby (or even the opposite)
- Grandma's house
- freshly baked chocolate chip cookies

What did you see in your mind's eye as you recalled each smell? With each image, did you have a shift in attitude?

Scent triggers a small movie to play in your mind that evokes more than memories and images of your surroundings. Fragrance is the *catalyst* that also brings up emotions and instinctive responses— responses that are linked to the situations surrounding the memory of the smell. This brief exercise underlines the link between smell and emotions, something you are usually quite unaware of.

Smells definitely do alter memory, emotion, and instinctive responses. I have a vivid memory of fragrance that altered my personal Chi. I was visiting Giverny, the home of the famous French Impressionist painter, Claude Monet. As I emerged from the house into the gardens, I was taken not only by the beautiful array of color and light that inspired his breathtaking works, but I was also overwhelmed by the fragrance. I began to cry as I walked along the garden path. There was no concrete emotion attached to the smells—I was just struck by the beauty of the scents, sights, and sounds. My Chi had been inspired by the lovely fragrances of Monet's living work of art.

Make your own catalyst. Mix an inspirational fragrance spray with one, or a blend, of these:

bergamot	frankincense	jasmine
benzoin	grapefruit	neroli
clary sage		rose

Caution: *Throughout the text, oils in italics should never be used during pregnancy.*

> The key to Fragrant Feng Shui is how you feel in an
> environment, and its association with fragrance.

Smells: Past, Present, and Future

Based upon your personal experience, each smell conjures up not
only a situation, but an emotional response. A wet wool sweater might
have elicited a memory of an endless day of boating, when rain
drenched you miles from the shore and you ached to be landside and
warm. Oranges may have sent you affectionately back to that freshly
squeezed glass that your grandmother would make and the love that you
felt for her as she prepared a special breakfast just for you.

 *Gratitude is one of the most magical of Feng
Shui tools. In gratitude for your "orange memories," why not eat an orange, enjoying the spray
of oils and orange essence as you peel it? Savor
its fragrance and taste, then ceremonially throw
a piece of the peel back to Mother Earth.*

Smells are powerful tools that evoke complex visuals and feelings
from the past. They also provide ongoing reference markers to the present. A whiff of pizza that interrupts your football game definitely snaps
you off the field and back into your living room, a hard-to-resist deli-
cacy! Scents do not just belong to the past and present—they can also
be used to shape the future.

The Essence of Feng Shui

Fragrance can be used to create the kind of life you have always
dreamed of. Just as scents can send you into the past, they can also be
used as a tool to link you to the future—one that you specifically create according to your dreams and visions. Smell can transport you into
the future by setting up a framework in which to move.

Most of us are already planning for our retirement. We have a game plan on how to save money so we can live comfortably. We have visualized where we would like to be living, and perhaps what hobbies we would like to cultivate. These are plans we are making for the future.

But life is for living now!

Most times we do not make these same kinds of plans for our immediate and mid-range future. We let the current of life carry us along. But we can make positive changes in our lives more frequently by using desire and intention. And, through linking the changes with fragrance, we can begin making subtle, wonderful improvements on a daily basis to live the kind of life we really want.

> *I am convinced that, as a little fairy told me, when you make the transition and leave this life, you are asked two questions: "Were you a good person?" To which you should be able to say YES! And, just as important, "Did you have a good time, living to the fullest and leaving nothing undone?" Again, your answer should be a resounding YES!*

Setting Goals—Let's Do It!

Organizational gurus, the masters of creating Fortune 500 personalities, beg us to make lists of our goals, which is all well and good, except that most of us can never find the list. Smell is a much easier and more powerful tool for us to chart our future right now.

You can use fragrance in the present to link yourself to a visualization of a future you would like.

The beauty of using fragrance to improve your future lies in its simplicity.

Ask your nose to help you pick one! What smells good? How does it make you feel?

With Fragrant Feng Shui, you will choose an aroma with specific overtones that gives you positive feelings and emotions. You then link the smell to the visualization (mental picture) of what you want to create in your life. Then, each time you use this scent sprayed in your home or on your body, that link will be renewed, and you will evoke the visualization of your goal. You are then on your way to creating it.

Goal-Setting Exercise:

Ah, but now the dilemma creeps in. You say to yourself, *This sounds great, and easy, too. It's just that I don't have any specific goals, at least none that I can think of.* The task of defining your goals is not difficult. The only tool you need is your complete honesty. You must ask yourself what it is *you* really want out of life, not what society, family, and friends demand from you.

Go to a quiet place where you won't be disturbed, and play some contemplative music if you'd like. Since lavender is a great essential oil to use for visualization and regeneration, give the area a spritz with the lavender spray you've already made up. Or, this might be a good time to add to your repertoire of smells and experiment with another oil, perhaps from the ones below.

Visualization and Regeneration Oils:

roman chamomile   lavender   neroli   rose

Quiet your mind. Let all your thoughts of the day slip away. Now move your attention down into your body. Feel yourself breathing. Spend a few moments just quietly observing the cycle of your breath going in and out. Then, staying with your breath, begin to feel calmness and peace radiating out from your stomach area.

What does this peace really *feel* like? Capture this feeling and record it in your mind. This is your natural state. This is how you should feel about your life. When you think of your job, you should feel this peace; when you think of your relationships, you should feel this peace; when you think of your family, you should feel this peace. This goes for the rest of the areas of your life, too.

If you feel a knot in your stomach when you think of your job, it means you are not feeling peace in this particular area of your life; it means that there are new goals for you to set. Please don't panic (it's not your natural state!). This isn't about you not measuring up to an idealistic state; it is about shifting your life on a daily basis to bring yourself closer and closer to this inner balance.

Go through each area of your life—your job, your family life, your spiritual practice, your intimate relationship, your friendships, and your community work—and ask yourself the questions below. Be completely honest.

1. Does it make me happy? (There isn't a person walking the planet who doesn't have ups and downs.) If not, ask: What would truly make me happy? What is stopping me from making the necessary changes?

2. Am I able to express myself honestly and fully? If your answer is no, then there is some aspect of your life where you are not able to speak your truth; it means that you are not living up to your potential.

3. Are my talents being used on a daily basis? Hiding your light under a bushel doesn't serve anyone. You are not releasing your creative energy (which then is usually bottled up inside as anger), and the world is not able to benefit from the gift you were born to contribute to humanity.

4. Do I feel fulfilled? This is a tricky question. Being fulfilled does not mean being successful in the eyes of society. It means quietly living each activity to the fullest, whether that be washing dishes, constructing a new building, or bonding with your new baby.

5. Does this area of my life have a connection to the greater good of the planet? Every action you take has repercussions throughout the web of life. Make sure that each area of your life is contributing to the betterment of yourself, your fellow humans, and Mother Earth. If you destroy what is around you, you destroy yourself.

Don't worry what your responses sound like. You have been honest, so the answers will provide you with fuel for change. Start plotting your steps to make that change. For example, perhaps you are unhappy with your job as a bank executive because you *truly* want to be a musician, but you can't afford to quit your job because you have a family to support. That's okay, but what are you going to do to move yourself toward your goal over the long term? Can you join a band on the weekends? Can you study after work with a maestro to improve your playing?

If you don't start moving toward the goals that really matter to you, you will never experience living in peace. Start today. Go back over each of the areas and plot your strategy for change. How are you going to take steps to reach that inner peace?

Now comes the fun part. Begin linking these goals to smells that please you. If your goal is to start taking a martial arts class that will help you become more focused in your spiritual practice, what fragrance would remind you of that goal every time you spray it? How about the fresh smell of pine? Or the vibrant smell of lemon? What if you want to start your own business? What fragrance would smell like a growing and flourishing business? Perhaps it might be a rich and full smell like that of a rose, or maybe the crisp smell of eucalyptus.

As you have seen, smell is subjective; you can link your goals to any smell you want. Once your goal is linked to a smell, every time you experience that smell, it becomes a subliminal trigger to help keep you on the path to realizing your objective. The key is to trigger your goals with a scent. We will explore how to link these goals to specific scents that are also linked with the energy centers of our bodies and homes in chapters 6 and 7, but for now, just practice getting your nose in shape!

Perhaps your goals are a bit clearer to you now and you feel charged about changing them. What is it, though, that really creates change, leading to a more fulfilling life? Let's consider what it is that creates all life situations.

Awareness of Thought

Experience everything around you—the chair you are sitting on, the bottle of fragrance in front of you, even this book that you're holding. None of these things existed until its creator thought, *Gee, I bet I could make a really great...(chair, fragrance blend, book) that would look something like...(visual image).* With thoughts, the creative process is set in motion: the furniture maker sits down to make some sketches and measurements, the perfumer formulates his/her recipes, or I sit down to the computer. Each object or creation was first a thought in someone's head—it could be yours!

This goes for abstract, nonphysical *things* as well. Consider your education. First it was a thought in your head: *Well, I would really like to be a (doctor, mechanic, pilot, artist), so I will go to school and practice until I become one.*

What surrounds you in your life, whether you are conscious of it or not, was first a thought, a thought without form.

In recognizing what you desire in life, you have taken the first step in its creation.

When you are aware of this underlying process, you can start to consciously use this information on a daily basis to create the kind of life you truly want. When you link this creative process to fragrance, you give yourself a tangible tool to help facilitate your growth. The fragrances you will be using to help you link your Feng Shui changes can be created by you.

Essential Oils—The Origins of Good Scents

There is sometimes confusion about exactly what essential oils are and how they work. You have already been playing with them and discovering their properties, but to better understand the tools you are using, it's helpful to explore their background, composition, and fragrant power.

Although we tend to associate "scentual" Chi with blossoms and flowers, essential oils are extracted from different parts of the plants—whether it be the leaf, blossom, resin, bark, root, seed, berry, rind, or flower. A single plant, like the bitter orange tree, can produce different oils from distinct parts: sweet-smelling orange oil is extracted from the fruit peel, petitgrain from the leaves and twigs, and neroli from the blossoms.

The natural substance that is extracted through a distillation process can be up to 100 times more powerful than its dried herb counterpart. The substances that make up the oil are a complex array of chemicals, some of which we have yet to fully understand. These chemicals work on the body at the cellular level and can assist in vital healing and restorative functions.

Aromatic oils are much more than pretty smells; they have the power to balance and heal the body, mind, and spirit.

The workings of these powerful essences is nothing new. The use of essential oils is both an art and a science that dates back at least 6,000 years. Ancient civilizations used aromatic oils in religious ceremonies, purification rituals, and for healing. Egypt is well known for using such aromatic oils as cedar and myrrh for embalming. Egyptians also had an advanced knowledge of ritual perfume use for both religious ceremonies and spiritual enlightenment. In China, the medicinal use of herbs and aromatics is recorded in medical texts dating back to 2000 B.C. Ayurveda, the health tradition of India, uses oils and blends that have been used for the past 60 centuries.

Western Europe also has a tradition of using aromatic oils and herbs. The aromatics of Arabia flowed into the West during the Crusades; rose water became one of the most popular scents of the time. During the plagues of the Middle Ages, the famous physician and prophet Nostradamus treated thousands of the afflicted with his "rose pills," which contained rose, aloe, cypress, iris, and cloves. During the Renaissance, aromatics remained a staple of pharmacies to combat epidemics. Perfumery and distillation industries flourished, especially in Grasse, France, which remains to this day an important fragrance center.

With the advent of the scientific revolution, synthetic duplicates were developed that helped launch the modern drug industry. Pharmaceutical companies learned quickly that there was great profit in the business of imitating, packaging, and selling what Mother Nature did perfectly well. In fact, the majority of modern medicines are chemical copies of naturally occurring plants. In the process of slick 20th-century marketing, these companies have sold people on trusting the synthetic duplicates over what Nature produces.

Fragrant Chi

Synthetic duplicates of essential oils are inorganic substances that do not contain Chi. In the plant realm, where essential oils are derived, Chi is the life force that transforms the Chi of the sun, the Chi of the Earth, and the Chi of water from the heavens into the plants themselves. Chi is not born and never dies; it is in constant flux. Therefore, when you use essential oils, the life energy of each plant, once universal Heaven and Earth Chi, is transformed into your Chi.

**Essential oils are gifts from Mother Nature that hold
the distilled essence of Heaven and Earth Chi.
Fragrance is Chi that smells good!**

You can see that fragrance is part of the universal cycle of Chi, moving and transforming whatever it comes in contact with. It is tangible evidence that nothing in the universe is separate—we are all wonderfully part of the same universal energy.

We are one another's brothers and sisters!

When we do not use pure essential oils, we are missing out on the life-force element of these elixirs. Scientists can imitate the smell, but they cannot reconstruct the complex chemical makeup of the oil and its Chi—its aliveness. Copies of essential oils lose the true scope of their therapeutic benefits. The moral of the story? Use only 100 percent natural essential oils. Natural essential oils have therapeutic value with the ability to balance and heal the body, mind, and spirit. Their fragrant Chi has a powerful, transformative effect on all three levels of being. Each oil has distinct properties and characteristics that influence us in different ways.

Body

These essential oils work wonders on your body!

circulation:
cypress, lemon (tonics);
lavender, ylang ylang (stress and hypertension);
black pepper, rosemary (stiff joints and muscles)

digestive system:
roman chamomile, *fennel,* orange, *peppermint* (indigestion)

endocrine system:
roman chamomile, *clary sage,* jasmine, lavender (menstrual cramps); *black pepper,* rose, patchouli, ylang ylang (aphrodisiacs)

immune system:
basil, eucalyptus, lavender, tea tree (warding off colds/flu);
eucalyptus, lemon, tea tree (fever reducing)

nervous system:
bergamot, roman chamomile, lavender, sandalwood (stress);
basil, jasmine, *peppermint,* ylang ylang (nervous fatigue)

respiratory system:
eucalyptus, pine, sandalwood, thyme (good for coughs and colds);
frankincense, myrrh (chills, congestion)

skin: tea tree oil, lavender, lemon (antiseptics);
roman chamomile, geranium, lavender, rose, neroli (healing)

Caution: *Throughout the text, oils in italics should never be used during pregnancy.*

The effects that these oils have on the body can be analgesic, antibacterial, antidepressant, anti-inflammatory, antiseptic, antiviral, deodorizing, expectorant, sedative, and more. They work on all the major body systems: circulatory, respiratory, digestive, immune, and nervous, among others. They also have the ability to be, like lemon balm, stimulating to certain systems while relaxing to others.

When essential oils are absorbed through the skin through bath or massage, they work through the body's chemistry by moving through the muscle tissue and on into the bloodstream. They are then distributed throughout the body and into the vital organs and tissues. There they work on the various body systems, depending on their chemical makeup.

How Essential Oils Affect Body and Mind

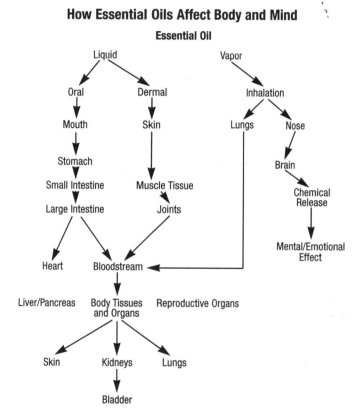

Essential oils can be used to treat a gamut of health disorders, from diarrhea and epilepsy to high blood pressure and insomnia. Many of the oils are multifunctional. Lavender oil can treat a wide array of problems, such as athlete's foot, acne, burns, asthma, throat infections, nausea, headaches, hypertension, and sciatica—and this is just a partial list![5]

---

[5] I invite you to learn more about fragrance and health in the many books that are available.

There is another important function that aromatic oils serve in our highly stressed, modern world. As living Chi, or vital Earth energy, they contain specific bio-electric properties that, when sprayed in the air, can balance, neutralize, and de-stress our living spaces.

This is really more straightforward than it sounds. Our bodies are made up of cells that carry electrical charges, which in turn create a direct-current energy field or *aura* around the body. Our modern environment is filled with electrical devices, power lines, microwaves, and computers that all operate on alternating currents, a pattern that is disharmonious with our own. So, modern living means that our bodies are functioning literally on a different wavelength from everything in our surroundings. This causes imbalances and stress in our bodies.

When sprayed or diffused into a room, essential oils have a Chi-altering effect. They change the *note* of the atmosphere, making it more calming, stimulating, and/or reenergized—depending on the characteristics of the specific oil used. Additionally, the aromatic oils add negative ions (which are beneficial) to the air; this shifts the frequency of the atmosphere that has become overloaded with positive ions released by electrical devices.

Mind

The nose is a fast track to moods and well-being. Improve yours with:

happiness: *basil,* benzoin, geranium, lime, and orange

energy and mental alertness: *basil,* benzoin, *black pepper,* eucalyptus, lemon, *juniper,* and *peppermint*

joy: neroli, rose, sandalwood, and ylang ylang

peace: bergamot, roman chamomile, frankincense, myrrh, and rose

confidence and self-esteem: cypress, ginger, grapefruit, jasmine, lavender, pine, sandalwood, and vetiver

creativity: cypress, geranium, iris, *juniper,* and sandalwood

stimulation of the conscious mind: *basil,* benzoin, *peppermint,* petitgrain, sage, and *thyme*

Caution: *Throughout the text, oils in italics should never be used during pregnancy.*

We have touched on the powerful effect that fragrance has on the mind. One whiff and our mind becomes a movie screen. Each oil or scent stimulates our smell receptors at a different frequency, which sends a distinct message to the brain. It is here that we receive the subtle messages that we have stored in relation to the scent.

Essential oils also have a powerful influence on our emotions and states of mind. Our olfactory nerves connect directly with the limbic system in the brain—the part concerned with memory and emotion. This is why a smell has such an instantaneous and profound effect on us.

Why not, then, consciously alter our moods with fragrance? Since the brain is so flexible, perhaps a euphemism for how little we understand its workings, it can be influenced by using fragrance.

You can use fragrance as a positive link between
your emotional center and your consciously created goals.

Spirit

Explore your spiritual side with these oils:

self-awareness: *clary sage,* cypress, sandalwood, and ylang ylang

spirituality: *atlas cedarwood,* frankincense, iris, myrrh, and sandalwood

magical energy: orange, *nutmeg,* and ginger

love: cardamom, rose, and ylang ylang

purification: eucalyptus, *fennel, juniper,* lemon, neroli, *peppermint,* and petitgrain

meditation and psychic awareness: roman chamomile, myrrh, *nutmeg,* and sandalwood

Caution: *Throughout the text, oils in italics should never be used during pregnancy.*

Aromatic oils have been used since recorded history for religious ceremonies and rituals. The ancients had a deep understanding of the inherent connectedness of all creation. Aromatic oils and incense were their earthbound link to the spiritual realm.

Fragrance was also used to link people with their deities. Temples in India were made out of fragrant sandalwood. (Not only did the Hindus use their version of Feng Shui, called *Vastu Shastra,* to build their sacred structures, but at the same time, as a matter of course, they also incorporated fragrance.) Sacred Vedic literature coded aromatics' use for worship as well as for therapeutic purposes. Fragrant incense was burned in Egyptian temples to call upon the spirits, and the Jews had ceremonial cleansing rituals for the body in which essential oils played the starring role.

The ancients provide us with the wonderful understanding that there was no separation between spirituality, healing, and day-to-day living. Fragrant Feng Shui!

The ancients realized that everything in Nature played an integral part in the cycle of life. They needed only to watch a sunflower, nautilus shell, or fern grow to understand how the universe worked its mysterious, interconnected wonders through natural sacred geometry.

Chi spiraled up from the ground, which made the plants unfold in their own blossoming spirals,[6] which in turn reached for the sky to be nurtured by the Chi that rained down from the movement of the planets as they spiraled in the Milky Way.

The Three Levels of Human Beings

Body, mind, and spirit are integral pieces of the whole person. Without harmony in one of these levels, the others would suffer as well. Feng Shui is about keeping these three levels in balance. Physical illness and problems that crop up in your life are related to imbalances in specific energy centers of your body and your home.[7]

Essential oils can heal and balance these three levels. They can be used according to the sacred geometric concept that the microcosm of the plant reflects the macrocosm of humans. The use of specific oils on designated areas of the body follows a generalized three-tiered pattern.

The Effect of the Relationship Between Humans and Plants:

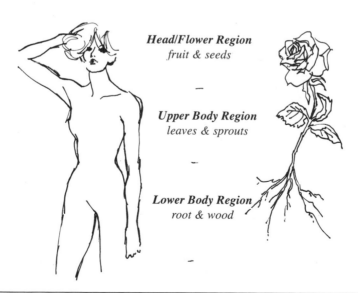

Head/Flower Region
fruit & seeds

Upper Body Region
leaves & sprouts

Lower Body Region
root & wood

---

[6] Plants' precise geometric leaf distribution, called phyllotaxy, follows a spiraling mathematical progression called the Fibonacci series. It is interesting to note that the spiral is also repeated on the tissue, cellular, and molecular levels of plant growth.

[7] Read the story about the Throat Chakra in chapter 5.

The oils and herbs that are derived from the root of plants are used on the systems of the lower body. Ginger has been used for centuries to enhance digestion. Hildegard Von Bingen, the 12th-century healer and mystic, wrote of its properties as an aphrodisiac, stimulating the *potency* of older men. The midsection of plants or their leaves are used to treat the upper body region. Eucalyptus leaves and twigs are distilled and used for coughs, colds, bronchitis, and chest infections. The fruits and seeds as well as blossoms are used for the head region and for more spiritual, *heady* pursuits. Jasmine is used to treat eye infections; neroli or orange blossoms treat depression and insomnia.

This three-layer division gives guidelines for the focal point of healing that a particular plant has. This is not to say that this is a cut-and-dried system. Each essential oil works on many different levels. For example, ginger also has curative powers for coughs and colds, which affect the upper body. Experienced aromatherapists have extensive knowledge in all the oils' uses. But for us laypersons, this gives a good basis on which to build our knowledge of fragrance.

Don't forget that body, mind, and spirit are connected. Use these oils to keep all three in sync:

| benzoin | geranium | lavender | vetiver |

The Symbolism of the Plant

As well as being chemical healers, plants, flowers, and their essences are also very powerful symbols used to connect humans to the cosmos. When we explore the symbolic significance of plants, we begin to see how we can use essences for our own transformation.

For example, since ancient times, frankincense has been associated with the sun.[8] It was and is used to evoke the essence of the solar deity,

---

[8] The symbolic correspondence of essences to planets, gems, colors, days of the week, and much more is well documented. Research into this field can be helpful in your symbolic and ritual use of fragrance, which we will explore in chapters 7 and 8.

whether it be named Apollo or Osiris. Frankincense was one of the three gifts of the Magi to the infant Jesus, and the Catholic Church to this day uses it in the language of symbolism to invoke their solar god, Christ. When you use frankincense, you can invoke its ancient meaning to create a psychological link to your solar potential and creativity. Isn't it only natural that fragrance, with such powerful symbolism, become an important addition to traditional Feng Shui?

The plant itself has also been a very powerful symbol throughout the ages. The tree has been worshiped in all native cultures. It embodied the cycle of all life as it moved through the seasons blossoming, giving fruit, dropping its leaves, and then going dormant for the winter. It was also believed to hold creative Divine energy that could be accessed by those who had the knowledge. Creation myths throughout the world speak of a World Tree, or Tree of Life. They believed that it represented perfect harmony and humans' ability to rise from their denser material roots to the higher spiritual realm.

The tree is a symbol of the growth of human potential.

The Norse had the Yggdrasil, or World Tree; Biblical accounts place the Tree of Life in the center of the Garden of Eden. The fruits that hung from it represented the goal of spiritual development, the Tree of Knowledge, and inner wisdom. The Kabbalists also had a Tree of Life that contained the full range of human experience. All that human beings were capable of becoming, was arranged on this tree. It is with this powerful symbol of a living and growing tree that we begin exploring our own personal potential. When the knowledge that the tree contains is incorporated with Feng Shui and fragrance, we can attain balance and harmony in our lives.

Good Scents

Facial:

For a deep-cleaning facial, first open up the pores using 2–3 drops per 2 cups water (or in a steamer). Place towel over head and enjoy!

Facial Mask:

Next, add 3–5 drops to clay, yogurt, or avocado. Put your feet up and relax for 20 minutes.

Facial Oil:

Then, moisturize with 5–10 drops in a 30 ml (1 oz.) carrier oil specific to your skin type.

Dry Brush:

Apply 1–3 drops to a natural bristle brush.

Hair/Scalp:

To condition or protect hair from the elements, mix 15–20 drops in 30 ml (1 oz.) of carrier oil.

Refresher:

Great to get a fragrant charge—use 5–10 drops of selected oil in distilled, purified, or spring water for facial toner or body wrap. To refresh a room, use 18–40 drops. Always shake, then spray.

Body Wrap:

First make a "refresher bottle," generously spray towel, wrap body with plastic sheet and blanket, then relax 20 minutes. Ahh!

Caution: *Throughout the text, oils in italics should never be used during pregnancy.*

Applications

CHAPTER 3

The
Tree of Life

If your intention is to enhance your life while incorporating fragrance that comes from plants and trees, it is only logical that your first symbol of Fragrant Feng Shui would be the Tree of Life. The ancient Kabbalists used the sacred symbol of the tree as a map of the cosmos, and of human beings. The ten universal archetypes that grew on the tree were connected by Chi and formed a pattern that could reveal the secrets of existence. The Tree of Life became a guide for raising consciousness for personal and universal evolution. Isn't this also the purpose of Feng Shui—to cultivate your personal energy and manifest your desires for a better life for yourself and your world?

The Tree of Life is the symbol of the
universal workings of Creation.

As you look at this tree, you see that it is rooted at its base and then branches out with ten hanging fruits, looking ready to be picked and bitten into. Can't you just smell its magical fragrance? And in essence, that is what you must do if you want to understand the mysteries that it holds. Each of the spheres contains a mystery, an essence, of what makes you human. They show you how you can reach the depths of your humanness rooted in the earth and the heights of your Godliness that reaches up to the sky.

You can enhance your life by working up through the branches of the Tree of Life.

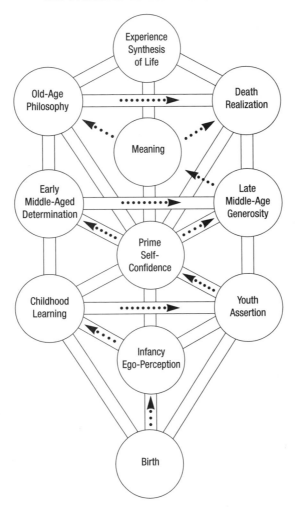

Personal Chi Evolution

Personal awareness, like that created as you move through the lessons of the Tree of Life, is the basis for effective Feng Shui. If your goal is to change your life for the better and to explore your potential, the Tree of Life can provide you with a road map. It is a tool for greater personal understanding, which then magnifies your Feng Shui manifestations. When you know where you are going, it is much easier to understand the appropriate Feng Shui adjustments you need to make to help you achieve your goals.

Sweet orange tree essential oil, which vibrates with happiness, joy, and contentment, is a perfect fragrance to celebrate the new blossoming evolution as you move up your own personal tree of success.

The Birth of the Tree of Life

The Kabbalah is a mystical system of knowledge about the origins of life and our place in the universe. The Tree of Life is a Kabbalistic symbol that shows the distilled essence of these teachings. The origin and age of the Kabbalah is unknown, although stories abound of its birth. Some claim that these sacred teachings were imparted by messenger angels to the patriarchs of the Bible from Adam through Moses and down to David. Others say that during Moses' third ascent to Mt. Sinai, God instructed him in the mysteries of the Kabbalah. Whatever its origin, the teachings were passed by word of mouth until written down in 13th-century Spain in a book called Zohar (The Book of Splendor).

Although its roots are ancient, the Kabbalah remains a vital tool for helping us make sense out of what our true mission is. It can act as a mirror that helps us see how body, mind, and spirit are balanced during our ascent into perfection. We can use the Kabbalists' Tree of Life to explore the basic ideas behind their teachings and to integrate them into our lives.

The Tree of Life is a pattern of life energies, a method of exploring the outer regions of inner space.

The Grand Design

In order to understand the Tree of Life, we must look at the basic tenets of the Kabbalah.[9] It states that the Original Force—God, Energy, Light Force, Divine Essence, Chi—was and is good and whole, and

---

[9] The Kabbalah elaborates much more on the voluntary emptying of the vessel and various other stages that complete the concept of sharing and receiving. Additionally, I find the Kabbalah to be all-encompassing. It is a symbol of cosmological workings, and much like astrology, numerology, elemental representations, and personality archetypes, it can be incorporated into Feng Shui.

embodies the attribute of sharing. As the Creator had only the desire to share, He created a vessel that was without limits to receive all that he had, and that was humankind. Our existence was created so that the dance between the desire to share and the desire to receive could be played out. We are the limitless vessels that receive all the Creator has to share so that we in turn may also be Creators by sharing what we have. Existence is sustained by the continuous cycle of giving and receiving.

Ah! Unlimited possibilities for giving and receiving!

Giving and receiving is about abundance.
Make two spritzer bottles of abundance oil
and give one to a friend:

basil	ginger	*nutmeg*
patchouli	pine	sage

This is our model for living, as well as the underlying purpose of Fragrant Feng Shui—to create unlimited potential for giving and receiving.

We must keep in mind this very important element of this cycle of life: We can be in harmony only when the desire to receive on all levels—physical, emotional, and spiritual—is in balance with the desire to share on all levels.

Harmony is as close as a spritz of
these essential oils:

roman chamomile	lavender	rose
clary sage	geranium	

Caution: *Throughout the text, oils in italics should never be used during pregnancy.*

Don't plants do this naturally?
They receive Heaven and Earth Chi and
share it as food and oxygen.

Perfect Kabbalistic Fragrant Feng Shui!

We were created as empty vessels that were meant to receive, but we must be careful not to fall into the trap of only wanting to receive. This is evident in our world today as we try to fill our vessel, that internal void, with material goods. But this was not the intention of the Creator. While desire and receiving things are certainly part of Earthly delights and our birthright, as well as part of a good Feng Shui experience, all the possessions and money in the world will not fill that void of the heart. The intention of the Creator was to pour life force into the vessel so that it could be shared with others. Then, by the act of sharing, we ourselves could be Creators.

When we share, we put the energetic cycle
in motion to be able to receive again.

Our apparent loss in the act of sharing is compensated for on the energetic level, and we are now open to receive. If our only desire is to receive, the wheel stops spinning and our lives do not evolve.

The Seed of Life

The Kabbalists use the organic symbol of the Tree of Life for many different reasons. Apart from creation story mythology, we can also understand that it is an important symbol of growth as well as individuality. Every tree grows according to sacred geometry—its seed puts down roots, and as it gains energy from its surroundings, it is able to push through the darkness and reach out through the ground into the light.

According to the Kabbalists, the seed contains the two intrinsic elements of creation—the desire to share and the desire to receive—that are beyond space, time, and motion. When this seed is subjected to the constraints of our physical world of space, time, and motion, the seed germinates and reveals its separate and dualistic parts.

The concept of the inherent duality of life abounds in philosophies around the globe. The Chinese concept of *yin,* the passive receptor; and *yang,* the active creator, fits this same mold.[10] The Mayans had Hunab Ku, whose symbolic representation is very close to the yin/yang iconography. Pythagoras used a list of ten pairs of opposites, which taken together, were the whole of the "law of opposites."[11] The hermeticists used the scientific terminology of the electrical, masculine/yang force and the magnetic, feminine/yin force. Like the Kabbalah, each one of these philosophies is based on the same understanding:

**One element imparts, and one receives,
while together they are the all-embracing unity of creation.**

**Here are a few essential oils that are
derived from seeds, to help you
"plant seeds for a new beginning":**

coriander   *fennel*   *nutmeg*

Caution: *Throughout the text, oils in italics should never be used during pregnancy.*

As the seed then germinates and reveals its duality, it uses the Chi that moves through the universe, which is being shared by the Creator, to grow. As it develops into a tree, the fruit it bears becomes both the source of knowledge and Chi, and the vehicle by which to share it with others.

The Vessels

The Tree of Life contains ten vessels of energy or fragrant fruits of life called *sephiroth.* These vessels are seen as the vehicle by which the particular energy they contain was brought from the metaphysical realm into our physical universe. Taken in another light, the sephiroth have sometimes been described as mini power stations through which

---

[10] See chapter 5, pg. 76.
[11] It is said that those who invented the Tree of Life were inspired by Pythagoras. And why should that be surprising? He was the master of sacred universal mathematics.

Chi flows and is diluted so as to become usable on the physical plane.[12] As a whole, these ten sephiroth are seen as the human archetype, the Universal Human.

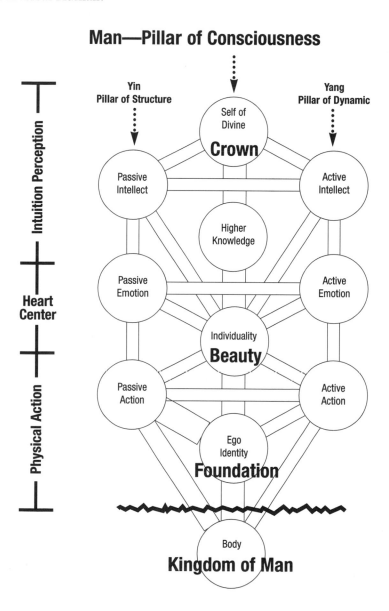

[12] This closely matches the description of the function of the Chakras as explained in the next chapter.

41

The ten vessels of energy are arranged in three pillars. The sephiroth on the right pillar have the qualities of imparting or sharing and are positive/yang, while those on the left have the qualities of receiving and are negative/yin (negative and positive have nothing to do with good and bad, but are merely the dualities). The middle pillar represents harmony between the opposites and humans living in perfect balance. Later on, we will examine the main trunk of the Tree of Life and its relationships to the energy centers of our bodies and our homes.

Taking Root

This Tree of Life can be taken in the literal sense. It provides an overview of the ages of human beings. From incarnation into the physical world, it moves into infancy and the beginnings of perception. It grows through the learning and assertion of childhood and youth. The prime of life as well as middle age is focused on more emotional and abstract concepts. Old age brings into sharper focus the more spiritual aspects of life. Death and the ultimate transcendental synthesis of all life experiences occur at the very top of the tree.

**As you move up through the branches,
you watch your life grow.**

This symbolic tree can also be explored from a more esoteric level. Although highly complex in its philosophy, it can be clearly understood if you focus first on the main trunk. It is firmly planted at its base in the *Kingdom*. This is your Tree of Life firmly planted in the terrestrial kingdom, Earth. Moving up the trunk, you come to the *Foundation*, the stabilizing force. The next vessel of energy is *Beauty*, the love that abounds in your life. Ascending, you reach the shadowy vessel, *Knowledge,* the vessel of knowing how to speak your truth. This is the symbolic link between the ego and the higher self. At the top of the Tree of Life is the *Crown*. This is the vessel that receives the spark of Divine essence. It is through this sephiroth that you are able to grasp your own Godliness. It represents the higher self that is not yet fully realized, and is the source of inspiration, freedom, and enlightenment.

**Take root, take hold of yourself.
You can't blossom until then...so add some
root oils to your blossoming:**

ginger   vetiver   sweet orange

When experienced in steps, this Tree also helps us understand the central point of knowledge, that of love. When we use sacred geometry of the macrocosm/microcosm, the symbol of the Tree of Life as Universal Human is clear. The center of the tree, or *Beauty,* is also the heart center of human beings. It is from this place of heart that the lower, more material regions of our Earthly existence are transformed into the upper, more spiritually oriented regions.

The symbol of the Tree of Life is like our wonderfully fragrant plants that we saw divided into three parts. Body, mind, and spirit are integrated throughout the growth of the plant. The roots provide the physical stability and ground us in the material; they provide nourishment from Mother Earth. The leaves that radiate out provide the vehicle by which energy from the elements of the universe is filtered through love to give beauty or nourishment to others. The blossoms, with their delicate, almost celestial, qualities, are the link to that which is the indescribable essence of life and creation.

The plant then becomes both a symbol and a tool for us to balance body, mind, and spirit. We can use its symbolism to understand our own growth, and we can use its physical essence, its scent, to help us grow into our potential. In Fragrant Feng Shui, we link the symbolism and fragrance of the plant to the changes that we would like to make in our lives. These changes are manifested in the energy centers of our bodies—our primary vessel—and the energy centers of our homes—our secondary vessel.

43

Good Scents

Face Spray:

For a light moisturizer, hydrator, or "flower water," add 8–10 drops of oil to 120 ml (4 oz.) of purified, distilled, or spring water. For more nourishment, include 20 drops of jojoba oil. Always shake before using.

Oily Skin:

Use light, antiseptic and astringent oils such as tea tree, bergamot, lemon, and geranium in your astringents, moisturizers, and face sprays.

Dry Skin:

Use sandalwood, rose, and chamomile for sensitive skin in such nourishing carriers as avocado and evening primrose oils.

Mature Skin:

Use oils to stimulate cell growth and to slow wrinkles—try lavender, neroli, and frankincense in carriers rich in vitamin E, such as wheat germ and rose hip oils.

Perfume:

Dab sandalwood, rose, or jasmine straight out of the bottle.

Hair:

To condition hair, combine 60 drops in 100 ml (3^1/2 oz.) of nourishing olive, jojoba, or almond oil. Wrap with towel and relax for an hour.

Dandruff:

Use bergamot or tea tree in hair oil.

Caution: *Throughout the text, oils in italics should never be used during pregnancy.*

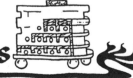

Beauty Tips

CHAPTER 4

The Energy Centers in Your Body

We have the potential to live in perfect balance. The Tree of Life, the definition of humans living in the cosmos, theoretically shows us how to live perfectly balanced between the law of opposites. But what if we are not perfect? What if there are things in our lives that we would like to change? Feng Shui is about making those changes in our homes. Since our bodies are our primary "homes," we can start enhancing our life with Feng Shui by making energetic shifts in our bodies.

Centers of Chi

Chakras are subtle energy centers in our bodies that transmit Chi between our bodies and our surroundings. Although the body has many hundreds of these concentrated energy vortexes covering all parts of our body, there are seven major Chakras that line the middle axis of our body.

These circles of energy are lined up along the spinal column of the body much as the main pillar of the Tree of Life holds the vessels of Chi that represent balance and harmony. In fact, the Chakra system is merely different symbology to view the same quest: to realize our true potential by developing our personal energy, our life force, our Chi.

The Chakras are a complete guide to understanding our primary vessel, our bodies.

The concept of Chakras is not new by any means. The Hindu culture recorded and worked with Chakras thousands of years ago. Their ancient texts refer to the flow of prana, or life force, through these energy centers within our bodies. For simplicity's sake, however, in this book I will refer to prana as *Chi*, the ancient Chinese, and Feng Shui, term for our life force. Although today we see ourselves as advanced in terms of scientific research and *energy exploration*, we are babes in the woods when it comes to understanding how Chi moves through our bodies.[13] Not so with the Indians—they used their extensive knowledge of the Chakras as an integrative tool for healing as well as for reaching spiritual enlightenment.

The Dance of Chi

If all this talk about energy exchange sounds foreign, we just have to remember our basic science class, where we learned that everything, regardless of shape, size, or even solidity is made of neutrons, protons, and electrons—with the latter two carrying positive and negative charges respectively. A chemical reaction is nothing more than a swapping of electrons and the charges they carry. Given this fact, we see that all interaction can be scientifically broken down into the dance of positive and negative charges, or the exchange of yin and yang Chi.

Our bodies are also pulsating with electrical charges. Each cell carries a charge; when combined, they create an energy field around the body. This energy body is constantly interacting with our surroundings whether we are aware of it or not. The Chakras are the body's method of streamlining this interaction. Each of the seven major centers carries a slightly different charge. This is why they are also depicted as the col-

---

[13] Shifting Chi within the energy vortexes and meridians is also the basis of acupuncture in Chinese medicine.

ors of the spectrum, vibrating from a low, red frequency at our base Chakra, to violet at our Crown Chakra. These centers act as miniature transmission stations; each Chakra deals with a different vibration of energy.

**Information from our surroundings
and from other people is filtered in the form
of Chi through the corresponding Chakra.**

This information on vibrational rates and how Chi is processed is important for understanding how the Chakras work and will also help us set the stage for our work with Feng Shui and essential oils. We know that essential oils have the ability to change the vibratory rate of what they come in contact with. When sprayed in a room, they add negative ions to the air, and balance the atmosphere. On the body, essential oils can have a similar effect. By using specific oils that resonate with a particular Chakra or Chi vortex, we are able to harmonize the body's energy. This is how we begin Fragrant Feng Shui.

To have a balanced body is to have a harmonious life.

The Sacred Wheel of Chi

Chakra means "wheel" in Sanskrit, and in effect, the body's Chakras are spinning wheels of Chi that are lined up along the spinal column. The circle is a symbol for the cyclical law; as the wheel rotates, the cycle is continuously renewed.[14]

**The circle is the symbol of wholeness and eternity;
the spiral is the continuum of Chi, and
planetary and personal evolution.**

---

[14] This spiral of energy up the spine is similar to the genetic spiral structure of DNA, the building blocks of life.

The Chakra System

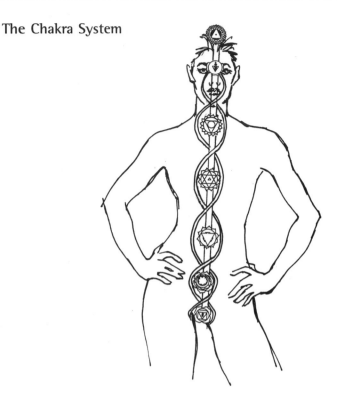

It is evident that the ancient culture of India was very much attuned to the symbolism and sacred geometry inherent in Nature and our bodies. It is not surprising then that when they are in balance, the Chakras are related to unfolding lotus blossoms—a full blossoming of their potential. What a great visual lesson for us.

**Chakras radiate creative energy out
into the universe like the blossom of a spiraling sunflower.**

The Chakras are in balance when they receive the optimum input and share the optimum output of energy. Receiving and sharing—this is the same lesson that the Tree of Life teaches us. The sacred geometry of the spirals of Chi, or Chakras, has brought us full circle to the teachings of the Tree of Life:

**Chakras are like individual wheels of life
receiving and sharing, sharing and receiving!**

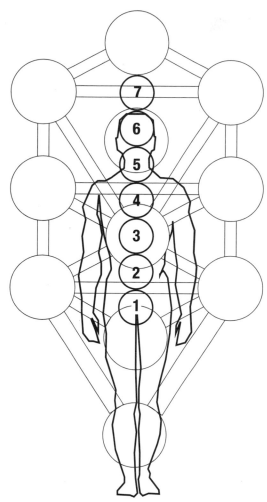

Look at the Chakras lined up along the spine and overlaid with the Tree of Life. Can you see yourself, your line of spiraling energy, mirrored in the main trunk of the Tree of Life? Both the tree and the Chakras are rooted at their base in Mother Earth. They move up through the heart center and are connected to the cosmos through the crown.

1. Root Chakra
2. Sex Chakra
3. Will Chakra
4. Heart Chakra
5. Throat Chakra
6. Third Eye Chakra
7. Crown Chakra

The Chakras

As with the vessels on the Tree of Life, the Chakras are a means of creating a full and balanced life. Each of the Chakras vibrates or spins at a different frequency, absorbing and radiating distinct types of energy. Their spin allows only like-kind energy through. If the Chakra is vibrating at its optimal level, it is exchanging life-affirming energy. If it is not, it attracts and imparts more of the same denser, destructive energy. The Chakras are open and receptive or blocked based on experiential factors, both karmic and circumstantial, that may occur during your life.

The key is to have all the Chakras vibrating at their optimal level, so you must *feed* them what they need. When you begin to understand the issues that fall under each Chakra's domain, you can better understand what types of changes you need to make in your life to get them functioning at highest efficiency.

The Chakra system is a means to integrate all vital life energies into your body so that you can become whole.[15]

Each Chakra relates to a certain set of physical, emotional, and spiritual issues; together they make up the complete package of personal Chi. As you read through the description of the Chakras, consider whether you see yourself in any of these concepts. Consider which of your Chakras may need to be enhanced with Fragrant Feng Shui so that your personal Chi will be in balance.

The Root Chakra

Function: survival, grounding

Key concepts: stillness, stability, money, safety, space boundaries

Body link: adrenal glands; as well as the legs, feet, bones, large intestines, and immune system

Associated ailments: weight issues—obesity, anorexia nervosa, bulimia; hemorrhoids, constipation, sciatica, arthritis, knee problems

Common addictions: alcohol, sex, compulsive cleaning

The first Chakra is located at the base of the spine at the perineum. It is the closest to the Earth, so logically, it is the grounding Chakra. It is your support and keeps you linked to Mother Earth and all her resources; it is like a plug into your terrestrial source of Chi. It is often referred to as the Root Chakra and vibrates to the color red.

Survival, making your own way in the world, and completing projects are some of the issues that the first Chakra deals with. Being able to provide for life's basic needs also falls under the first Chakra's domain.

---

[15] Wholeness is also a very important concept in life and in Feng Shui. We will explore it further with the Bagua, in the next chapter.

You receive Chi, abundance, and all that you need to survive from the earth. So issues of scarcity and greed are human inventions. This Chakra, then, becomes an energy center of trust, of believing that you will always be taken care of if you listen to your inner voice and Earth's voice about what you *really* need to survive, instead of what your consumer-driven society has led you to believe. This energy center is the foundation. By providing for your basic needs and safety, you give yourself the stable base on which to build your life and a healthy Root Chakra.

When you trust in the universe, you understand that there is enough and more for everyone.

Someone who has continual health problems or is always living day to day, wondering where their next meal or paycheck is coming from, has unresolved first-Chakra issues. Fear and attachment to security are also first-Chakra issues that are pervasive in our culture. Until we find balance within ourselves and trust that the universe will provide all that we need to reach our full potential, we will be pulled into the false sense of security that a materialistic society provides.

Let's look at an example of how fear crippled a woman who need-ed to start surviving on her own. In this book, I will be sharing several examples with you—stories of how Feng Shui analysis can both high-light the current problems one may be experiencing, and provide a path to their resolution. In the next few chapters, I will introduce the situa-tions or problems, then in chapter 8 you can read some of the solutions that I devised using Feng Shui. Now, however, I want to share with you my saddest Feng Shui (Root Chakra) consultation.

Janette was a beautiful 60-something "afternoon at tennis, bridge, or shopping with the ladies" divorcee. She lived with her working-professional, adult daughter in a very large, exclusive home. Her first words were: "I only have two more years of alimony, and I'd like to start positioning myself now." Sounded like a smart plan to me!

In her master bedroom, I saw the most bizarre thing I've seen in my 20-some years of being a professional interior designer. There were two chairs at the foot of the bed facing outward. Asking her why, she replied, "We used to watch the kids play in the pool." It was evi-

dent from that statement that she had changed nothing in her home for over 20 years. I then asked, with compassion (yet a certain amount of amazement), "Janette, has your life changed in the last 20 years? Are you the same person you were 20 years ago?"

The rest of the house confirmed her answer. Everything was dark (no Chi moving); all the art on the walls had been selected by her ex-husband, which she said she had never liked (I wasn't sure if she was talking about the art or him!); and the accessories throughout the home were gifts that had no significance. When I asked if there was anything in her home that she liked, she said, "Nothing." **[Feng Shui is about your home being a mirror of your life; what a powerful statement she had made with that comment.]**

Janette was only using two of the bedrooms, the kitchen and den (all Chi-less) in this huge home. Since its market value was $400,000-ish, I suggested that she sell it. Why pay all that extra expense of upkeep and cleaning? I advised her to move from this home that was a living monument to her old life (one that she didn't even like). With the money from the sale, she could buy her own, beautiful place that she loved for $150K, blow $50K on great new furnishings (donating everything that kept her tied to her old Chi-less life and ex-husband), and she would still have $200K to put in income-producing investments. She could really start living! Even her alimony would go further without the high overhead.

To get the plan in action and to have Janette stop wasting her life (the most precious of all gifts), I suggested some inexpensive Chi-moving Feng Shui (which would also motivate buyers). I called a few months later, and she said that she had done a few items, but stopped when the water heater had broken.

When someone stops making Feng Shui changes because a 25-year-old water heater stops working, it is evident that there is something bigger going on. Feng Shui adjustments start moving Chi, and changes start appearing. Perhaps, after so many years of being stuck in a rut, she could not deal with the changes that she saw happening around her. The water heater was a safe excuse to stop "having" to make changes. More than the issue of money, Janette's true fear was of letting go of the false security the house provided. She was afraid of taking charge of her own life and trusting that she could make a go of it. It still makes me sad to think of someone's life journey being short-circuited by fear.

<u>Essential Oils for the Root Chakra</u>[16]

Basil: money, purposefulness

Benzoin: physical energy

Black pepper: security, endurance, protection, physical energy, courage, stamina

Cinnamon: strength, practicality, steadfastness, physical energy, prosperity

Clove: protection, courage

Fennel: courage

Frankincense: courage, protection

Geranium: protection

Ginger: courage, physical energy

Juniper: protection

Nutmeg: physical energy, money

Orange: physical energy

Patchouli: physical energy, money

Pine: protection, physical energy, money

Vetiver: grounding, centering, strength, protection, money

Caution: *Throughout the text, oils in italics should never be used during pregnancy.*

ॐ   ॐ   ॐ

The Sex Chakra

Function: desire, pleasure, sexuality, procreation

Key concepts: feelings, empathy, emotional needs and boundaries, intimacy, creative procreation

Body links: sex organs, large intestine, bladder, pelvis, and lower back.

---

[16] Since most oils have many life-enhancing attributes, the oils listed for each Chakra and their energetic representations are only a sample of the possibilities.

Associated ailments: impotence; frigidity; uterine, bladder or kidney problems; lower back pain

Common addictions: sugar, food, alcohol, relationships

The second Chakra, the Sex Chakra, is located in the lower abdomen—in the genital or womb area—and vibrates to orange. The Chi that resides in this center is that of procreation; it is the center of sexuality, emotions, intimacy, desire, and pleasure. This Chakra oversees the transformation of sexual Chi into creation.

This is the Chi center of feeling. Feeling is also the best intuitive resource for all Fragrant Feng Shui and life. But our society values reason over feeling, so many of our true feelings get stuck in the Chakra without being released. When Chi gets stuck, it is stagnant, unable to generate or create.

> When we truly feel, then we are capable
> of creating what we really want.

In order to create the life you want, you need to *feel* what is really important to you and how you really want to spend your time and energy. These feelings must not be influenced by others' ideas of how you should feel or be. When you can shake off the need for social approval and for reason over feeling, you will be able to truly create what you desire.

The Root Chakra is about stillness, about grounding with our source, the Earth. The second Chakra is about polarity, duality, and movement. The Chinese yin/yang symbolism teaches that the universe is based on dualism: light/dark, day/night, female/male, from which ongoing creation is generated. This polarity has everything to do with relationships: You seek in others what is lacking in yourself. Through the other, like a reflection in a mirror, you search for understanding into your own missing elements and integrate them into your being.

This Sex Chakra deals with relationships and the concept of opposites attracting and creating a whole. Opposition is not bad, it just IS. Desire is the basis of movement; you seek to make yourself whole by finding the opposite and integrating it into your being. Marriage, relationships, and sexuality are the celebration of this concept, the joining of opposites to become one.

From the union of opposites, a greater creation is born.

This union also has everything to do with what we choose to create in our lives. We have been put here to learn to be Creators in our ability to receive and give back, just as the Kabbalah teaches. So when we understand the limitless abundance of the earth through our first Chakra, we are able to then create from this endless resource through our second Chakra.

Maryann was interested in a turnkey Feng Shui interior design project. She wanted new everything—a fresh look with new furnishings and new energy. It was obvious that she wanted a whole different outlook on life.

During the initial consultation, I found out why. Her husband, Steve, was the successful breadwinner with a very strong and intimidating personality. Maryann stayed at home to care for the house and the family. It became quite evident during our conversation that Steve viewed Maryann's job as less important than his. And if she didn't please him, in whatever capacity, he let his control of the purse strings do the talking. She thought she could fix it all through sex, but instead, Maryann developed a total lack of interest in intimacy with her husband, which filled her with guilt.

It was clear that the problems in their relationship as partners stemmed from living stereotypes that no longer work in today's world. They needed to come to terms with the lessons of the Sex Chakra: unifying their male/female sides, and learning about balanced emotional intimacy.

Unfortunately for Maryann, we never did the project because Steve conveniently found something unacceptable in my very standard design contract. This corroborated the fact that there were some other Chakra issues involved in their relationship ills. While Steve financially took care of household and family needs and money was abundant, it was "his" money. At the same time, he did not want Maryann to work outside the home.

I suspect that fear and security (Root Chakra) were the sources of Maryann's guilt. This guilt influenced her inability to stand up to him (Will Chakra), to be in her own power and say, "Stop controlling me. Either give me the money to make both our lives more beautiful [literally and figuratively], or I'll get my own job to pay for what I need and want."

I also questioned how Steve could be happy the way things were. The proper Feng Shui changes and a job for Maryann would create a sense of personal accomplishment and income for her, which would provide security, personal power, and most important, freedom to make choices. Perhaps Steve subconsciously knew the power that the Feng Shui changes would have and, through his own fear of change, refused to let Maryann follow through. Maryann, on the other hand, needed to stand up to a situation that no longer reflected the path that she wanted to walk. How sad to see stagnation when one of the few constants in life is change.

With Maryann's permission, I decided to use Feng Shui to enhance her lower Chakras. With this energetic shift, there would have been either a better balance in the couple's relationship, or she would have the self-confidence to move on. Either path would have provided her with personal growth and a happier life than she was currently leading.

 Permission: *I had such a strong urge to help Maryann start making those positive shifts in her life. But it is essential for a practitioner to get someone's permission before doing Feng Shui or any other energy work that creates shifts in life experience. No matter how good the Feng Shui practitioner's intentions are, until permission is given, it means that the recipient is not ready to receive these energetic shifts in their life. If the practitioner did otherwise, it would serve only to link their karma, which is harmful to them both.*

Essential Oils for the Sex Chakra

Atlas cedarwood: self-control

Bergamot: completeness, creativity

Black pepper: releases emotional blockage

Cardamom: love, sex

Cinnamon: warmth

Clove: creativity

Cypress: easing losses, creativity

Geranium: creativity

Ginger: warmth, sex, love

Grapefruit: emotional clarity, vigor, refreshment

Jasmine (E): sex, love

Juniper: creativity

Lemon: physical energy, creativity

Neroli (E): sex

Patchouli: sex, physical energy

Pine: self-forgiveness, acceptance, physical energy

Sandalwood: sex, creativity

Ylang ylang: sexuality, sensuousness, emotions

(E): These oils are either rare or require more plant material to make the oil; thus, they are considerably more expensive.

Caution: *Throughout the text, oils in italics should never be used during pregnancy.*

The Will Chakra

Function: will, power

Key concepts: personal will, power, energy, transformation, logic, laughter, joy, anger, balancing control over self versus others

Body links: pancreas and adrenal glands, as well as the stomach, small intestines, digestion, liver, spleen, and middle back

Ailments: ulcers, diabetes, hypoglycemia, intestinal problems, indigestion, liver problems, hepatitis, adrenal dysfunction, arthritis

Common addictions: food, caffeine, bread, details, compulsive cleaning

The third Chakra is in the navel area. Its color or vibratory frequency is yellow. Issues of personal will, self-esteem, self-confidence, and self-respect are the domain of the Will Chakra. It is here that you realize a deep sense of self and personal power.

This is the main focal point of personal Chi. If you learn to *move* through life from this place, you can never go wrong. One key to effectively using personal power, *your* Chi, is that it must always be aligned with Divine will; if not, it is merely misdirected energy that will ultimately do you harm. This is not to say that it is always easy to know what the Divine will is, but if you learn to trust that *gut instinct* — your personal power and will — even if it seems to go against what you have been taught, you will be walking the path you were meant to.

You must tap into your willpower to consciously channel change in your life.

If you have low self-esteem and think that you are unworthy or undeserving of all the wealth the universe has to offer, you give your power to someone else, which weakens you. When you use your power to create to your fullest capability, you are fueling the generative cycle[17] of wealth — for yourself and others.

Power also implies responsibility. You must be responsible for the decisions that you make. The energy of this Chakra allows you to break with debilitating societal patterns that keep you stuck in an occupation, in a relationship, or in activities that no longer serve you.

> We can now get a better understanding of the story I told in the first chapter about my insecurity with finances. It is my will (Will Chakra) that perpetuates my desire (Sex Chakra issue) to never fear financial insecurity (Root Chakra issue). All three work together, either generating or mitigating my bag-lady fears. When my Will Chakra is open, I am confident of my own capacity to keep myself in sound financial health, and the related fears never enter my mind.
>
> Clearly, all three "lower" Chakras revolve around physical reality. When we are grounded in the physical world, we are responsible to society and to our fellow human beings. It is difficult to explore the upper, more spiritual realms without first having our lives firmly planted.

---

[17] The generative cycle is critical in understanding Feng Shui; please see my book *Feng Shui Today*.

Essential Oils for the Will Chakra

Atlas cedarwood: assertiveness, confidence, self-image, self-control

Basil: assertiveness, decisiveness

Bergamot: confidence, assertiveness, creativity, performance

Black pepper: assertiveness, self-image

Cinnamon: directness, steadfastness

Coriander: assertiveness

Cypress: assertiveness, confidence, creativity, self-image

Fennel: assertiveness, confidence

Frankincense: self-image, assertiveness, performance, positivity, acceptance

Geranium: self-esteem, performance, positivity

Ginger: strengthening, confidence, assertiveness, courage

Grapefruit: confidence, performance, positivity, liberation, confidence

Jasmine (E): self-esteem, self-image

Lavender: performance, self-image

Lemon: health, healing creativity, positivity

Nutmeg: self-image

Orange: confidence, self-image

Pine: self-image

Rosemary: confidence

Sandalwood: self-esteem, self-image, creativity

Vetiver: positivity, self-esteem

Ylang ylang: self-esteem, self-image

(E): These oils are either rare or require more plant material to make the oil; thus, they are considerably more expensive.

Caution: *Throughout the text, oils in italics should never be used during pregnancy.*

❧   ❧   ❧

The Heart Chakra

Function: love

Key concepts: caring, compassion, trust, giving and receiving, being open to change, forgiveness

Body link: the thymus gland, as well as the heart, lungs, diaphragm, shoulders, arms, and hands

Ailments: heart disorders, high blood pressure, heart disease, lung disorders, asthma, breast cancer

Common addictions: cigarettes/nicotine, marijuana, etc.

The fourth Chakra vibrates to green and is located at the heart level. It is the center of heart Chi, midway between the three more physical Chakras below, and the three more esoteric Chakras above. This is the Chakra of unconditional love, trust, commitment, compassion, and hope. It also deals with their opposites: hatred, loneliness, anger, and bitterness.

During our Earth journey, the heart is the center of a spiral from which all of our actions should radiate out.

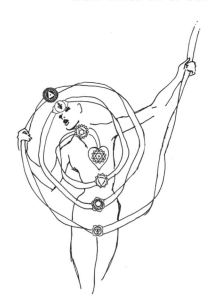

This concept of the spiral evokes the sacred geometry of the circle. This spiral of love energy not only balances us, but feeds the other Chakras as well. Love is the highest expression of all signs. Through the Heart Chakra, we are able to give and receive not only unconditional love, but all the abundance that life has to offer — friendship, love, laughter, and joy.

The Heart Chakra is our body's energetic healing center. It is connected to two minor Chakras in the hands. There are hundreds of subtle conduits for Chi that run throughout our bodies that the Chinese call *meridians*. These channels do not necessarily correspond to the blood or nervous system; instead, they are an independent network. There are meridians connecting the Heart Chakra to the Chakras in the palms of the hands. This is how hands-on healing takes place, or how even the touch of a loved one can calm and nurture us.

When the Heart Chakra is open, we are able to spontaneously heal ourselves and others.

Healing goes further than just that of the physical level; it also includes healing on the psychological and spiritual levels. One important ingredient for this kind of healing is forgiveness, also an important component of this Chakra. We live in a society that has perhaps forgotten its true meaning. We have created a legal system that is no longer focused on safety and justice for crime, but that is bloated beyond comprehension, overstuffed with people who want to get even.

You must begin to forgive, which does not mean condoning what the other did, but moving past seeing yourself as a victim. Revenge is reactive; forgiveness is proactive. And by forgiving, you fuel your own healing. In this way, you free yourself from the cycle of revenge. You can only function optimally from this Chakra when you forgive everyone—and when we all get good at this, we will change the world!

My favorite symbolic representation of the spiraling heart is the Fool card in the Thoth tarot deck.[18] The Fool is certainly a misnomer, as there is nothing foolish about him. He is also recognized as the Green Man or Dionysus, the god of Spring, both archetypes of new beginnings. The Fool's heart is opened, revealing a spiral with four turns. The four levels of the spiral are symbolic of the spiritual, intellectual, emotional, and physical dimensions that are ever-expanding energies of potential. It is through the heart that your aliveness reaches its capacity.

ॐ   ॐ   ॐ

---

[18] From the Thoth Tarot Deck, courtesy of Samuel Weiser, Inc.

Essential Oils for the Heart Chakra

Atlas cedarwood: comfort

Basil: happiness, peace

Benzoin: happiness, contentment

Bergamot: peace, happiness, joy

Black pepper: comfort

Cinnamon: happiness

Clove: healing, contentment, creativity, happiness

Coriander: love, healing, happiness

Cypress: healing

Eucalyptus: health, healing

Frankincense: joy, peace

Geranium: happiness

Grapefruit: joy, balance

Jasmine (E): peace, happiness

Juniper: healing, peace

Lavender: health, love, peace, contentment, restfulness

Lemon: health, healing, joy

Myrrh: healing

Neroli (E): joy, peace, contentment

Orange: contentment, happiness, joy

Petitgrain: joy, restfulness

Pine: understanding, patience, acceptance, healing

Roman chamomile (E): peace, joy

Rose (E): love, peace, sex, beauty

Sandalwood: contentment, joy, restfulness, healing

Spearmint: healing, protection during sleep

Thyme: health

Ylang ylang: peace, love, joy, contentment

(E): These oils are either rare or require more plant material to make the oil; thus, they are considerably more expensive.

Caution: *Throughout the text, oils in italics should never be used during pregnancy.*

The Throat Chakra

Function: communication, creativity

Key concepts: communication, listening, creating, speaking up

Body link: the thyroid and parathyroid, as well as the mouth, neck, shoulders, arms, hands

Ailments: throat/mouth ailments, sore throat, stiff neck, colds, thyroid problems

Common addictions: smoking, nasal inhalants, running (runners' high)

The fifth Chakra, radiating in bright blue, is located at the throat. It is the center of self-expression, speaking your personal truth, the power of choice, as well as judgment and criticism.

**The Throat Chakra is the energy center of personal will,
fully aligning with Divine will.**

The first three Chakras are about self-realization, recognizing who you are and what you are capable of. The Heart Chakra leads you into selfless love, and the fifth Chakra allows you to surrender,[19] not to someone else, but to the truth of who you are. You can then voice it to the world. You must communicate your gifts to the world and use your creativity to walk your path and accomplish your goals.

This is the Chi center of choice. Your personal power lies in your thoughts and actions. Every thought you have and action you take has repercussions in the world, so you must carefully consider your choices

---

[19] Boy, do I have a story for you in the next chapter!

63

and the impact they have. The concept of karma is actually straightfor-ward; situations reoccur in your life until you integrate the lesson and solve it in a way that is aligned with your higher self and Divine will.

This energy center deals with judgment and criticism. When you speak negative thoughts, you begin to create those negative forms in your life. When you criticize others, you are failing to realize that they are merely a mirror of your own shadow side. When you lie to others, you are also deceiving yourself—you block your true potential.

The Throat Chakra is also one of faith. Some consider it faith when you hand over your power to the Divine, but in fact...

Faith is nothing more or less than recognizing your divinity, knowing that you have the ultimate Divine power.

We have all had situations in our lives, such as the death of a loved one, the unexpected loss of a job, or an illness, that have plunged us into a darkness where personal power alone has not been enough to rescue us. It is in these times of crisis that we begin to understand and use our Divine will.

We tap into that force that is larger than ourselves, which simultaneously _is_ ourselves.

I have been telling you stories for each Chakra. Are you starting to see how they relate to your life issues? For the "upper" Chakras, I am going to combine them with the energy centers of your environment in the next chapter, so keep on readin'.

Essential Oils for the Throat Chakra

Atlas cedarwood: decisiveness, directness, conviction, integrity

Basil: clarity, decisiveness, clarity of thought

Cardamom: clarity

Cypress: generosity, directness

Frankincense: generosity, conviction, acceptance

Geranium: communication, acceptance, assistance

Grapefruit: generosity, communication

Jasmine (E): assistance

Juniper: conviction

Lavender: assistance, acceptance, integrity, directness

Lemon: communication, clarity of thought, acceptance

Neroli (E): forgiveness, understanding

Peppermint: decisiveness, communication, acceptance

Petitgrain: acceptance

Pine: forgiveness, directness, acceptance, understanding

Roman chamomile (E): generosity, forgiveness, communication

Rose (E): acceptance

Thyme: decisiveness, conviction, assistance

Vetiver: conviction, integrity

(E): These oils are either rare or require more plant material to make the oil; thus, they are considerably more expensive.

Caution: *Throughout the text, oils in italics should never be used during pregnancy.*

The Third Eye

Function: seeing, intuition

Key concepts: awareness, clairvoyance, psychic powers

Body link: the pineal gland, as well as the brain, nervous system, eyes, ears

Ailments: blindness, headaches, nightmares, eye strain, blurred vision

The sixth Chakra vibrates to indigo and is situated at the brow. This is your visionary Chakra that can propel your ideas out into the world in a form that may surprise even you. This is where perception occurs—ideas that seem to have no basis in your waking reality are integrated through this Chi vortex and made concrete—usable in the mundane world.

This is the gate of perception through which you see, hear, and experience things that have no rational explanation. You see without eyes, you hear without ears, and you *just know* something. Divine truth becomes clear and needs no explanation for you to simply know that it is right. This is also when synchronicity appears with greater frequency; events and people seem to coincide at exactly the right time—things just seem to fall into place.

When you can begin to act spontaneously on the intuitive information that you receive, you will greatly enhance the accuracy of your decisions and actions. You sense that you have tapped into a huge data bank of information that your rational mind has no way of accessing.

**When you are acting on your intuition,
you begin to foster a sense of inner peace and well-being.**

It is from here that you can visualize the kind of life you would like to live. Since thought creates, if you can begin to give visual form to your desires, you can then fill them with the Chi of creation through the Third Eye. This Chakra has a very concrete role in manifesting your Feng Shui desires. When you can *see* what you want to create, it begins to take form.

Essential Oils for the Third-Eye Chakra

Atlas cedarwood: concentration

Basil: conscious mind, awakening, clarifying

Benzoin: conscious mind

Black pepper: mental alertness

Cinnamon: alertness, focus

Clary sage: dreams

Clove: memory, focus

Coriander: memory

Eucalyptus: alertness, concentration

Fennel: focus

Grapefruit: alertness

66

Jasmine (E): psychic dreams

Juniper: alertness, focus

Lavender: conscious mind

Lemon: concentration, focus

Nutmeg: psychic awareness

Orange: concentration

Peppermint: conscious mind, alertness, concentration

Petitgrain: conscious mind

Roman chamomile (E): meditation, concentration

Rosemary: conscious mind, memory, concentration

Thyme: conscious mind

(E): These oils are either rare or require more plant material to make the oil; thus, they are considerably more expensive.

Caution: *Throughout the text, oils in italics should never be used during pregnancy.*

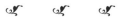

The Crown Chakra

Function: understanding

Key concepts: inner knowing, oneness, selfless service, spiritual love, bliss

Body links: the pituitary gland, as well as the central nervous system, muscular system, skeletal system, and skin

Ailments: depression, alienation, boredom, apathy

The seventh Chakra is at the crown of your head and vibrates with the color violet. This is your transcendental Chakra, the thousand-petaled lotus. Just as the Root Chakra was a plug into the Chi of Mother Earth, the Crown Chakra is your plug into the Chi of the cosmos. All that seems incomprehensible and unintelligible, all the concepts you see as bigger and grander than yourself, are accessible through this energy center. It is your link to God—Divine essence—the Chi of creation. Through this Chakra, you experience selflessness, humanitarianism, faith, grace, spirituality, and Divine bliss.

You gain enlightenment through this Chakra, which is just another way of saying that you are able to see yourself as whole.

It is the gate of consciousness, that force that fills you with the knowing of who and what you really are. When you are incarnated in this body, you take form and become material. But this is not the essence of who you are; this is just a transitory state. It is here that you learn what you truly are and what you are truly capable of. When you reintegrate yourself into that larger sea of energy, consciousness, or Divine Essence, you have then integrated all the lessons of the seven Chakras and are ready to meet new and unfathomable experiences.

Essential Oils for the Crown Chakra

Atlas cedarwood: spirituality

Cinnamon: psychic awareness

Clary sage: euphoria, calmness, dreams, self-awareness

Clove: self-awareness

Coriander: self-awareness

Cypress: self-awareness

Frankincense: spirituality, meditation

Geranium: self-awareness

Jasmine (E): spirituality, psychic dreams, self-awareness

Myrrh: spirituality, meditation

Roman chamomile (E): meditation

Sandalwood: self-awareness, spirituality, meditation

Ylang ylang: self-awareness

(E): These oils are either rare or require more plant material to make the oil; thus, they are considerably more expensive.

Caution: *Throughout the text, oils in italics should never be used during pregnancy.*

Evolution

We develop in the same way that plants grow and evolve. Plants depend on a strong root system and a firm stem to nourish the leaves. The leaves reach up for the sky to transform light into Chi. The blossoms are the crowning glory that interact with the other species — whether they be the birds or the bees or humans. Each portion of the plant is important to its health and growth.

If we are going to evolve on this planet and be happier in life, we must realize that the same applies to us. Each Chakra provides an essential function to the whole. The complete Chakra system is the key to personal evolution and to developing personal Chi. What the Kabbalah showed us on a more symbolic level, the Chakras teach us on a more physical level.

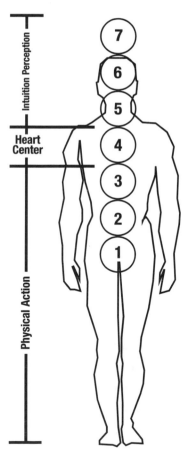

The center of the physical Chakra system, as in the Kabbalah, is love, the heart. The heart center opens us up to unconditional love and works as a transmutation center. This spiral of Chi allows the lower, more physical, aspects of our being to be transformed into the more spiritual. Survival of the first Chakra is no longer just a physical issue of getting by; it becomes an issue of spirituality as well. The Heart Chakra also allows us to use Divine energy and to pull it down into the real world. A deep understanding of the connectedness of all humans through the Crown Chakra helps us in our personal relationships of the second Chakra.

Each of the Chakras must be working at its optimum level. If we are not grounded through the Root Chakra, then we are without foundation, and everything we have built above it in the more spiritual centers will tumble. Or, if we cannot open ourselves at the Crown Chakra to inspiration, then we will never be able to see the larger picture, the interconnectedness of all humans. Start experimenting with your favorite oils based on the key words for each of the Chakras. Review the goals that you wrote down, and mix your oils to address both your goal and the Chakra(s) that it relates to.

As you can see, the energy of action in the more physical Chakras is transmuted through the heart center into intuitive energy and perception of the upper Chakras.

Through the Chakra system, you can see the body as a circuit in a larger energy plan. It is not about drawing energy up through the earth and out through your Crown Chakra to reach the highest heights, nor is it about reveling in the stream of consciousness you absorb from the universe and pulling it down through your body to merely enjoy Earthly pleasures.

Watch the plants! They get their Chi from below *and* above. It is the same for us. It is about plugging in at both ends and creating a kind of closed circuit in which the energy of the planet below and the universe above nurtures us equally. When we realize we are connected at both ends, we know we are not alone.

**We are plugged into Mother Earth and Father Sky.
What better help could we ever ask for?**

Each Chakra has a lesson for us to learn, and it is an ongoing process. If all our Chakras were in perfect working order, we would either be deemed living saints, or we would have connected into the next order of business and left the planet. So our Chakra system is an ongoing, living classroom. It assists us in transforming all those aspects of ourselves that separate us from other humans and our higher self. It will be an important tool for us to use in examining where we need to make changes in our lives. We can then use fragrance and Feng Shui adjustments to help us get our primary vessels, our bodies, glowing and growing.

Good Scents

Indigestion, Pain, Spasms:
Peppermint, roman chamomile, orange, lemon, *cinnamon,* lavender

Sinusitis, Coughs, Bronchitis:
Eucalyptus, pine, *thyme,* sandalwood

Colds, Chills, Congestion:
Benzoin, frankincense

Flu, Colds, Sore Throat, Tonsillitis:
Thyme, pine, eucalyptus, tea tree

Protection Against Colds, Flu:
Tea tree, *basil,* lavender, eucalyptus, bergamot, *clove, rosemary*

Reducing Fever, Temperature:
Basil, peppermint, thyme, lemon, *clary sage,* tea tree, eucalyptus

High Blood Pressure, Palpitations, Stress:
Ylang ylang, lavender, lemon

Poor Circulation:
Rosemary, eucalyptus, pine, *peppermint, thyme*

Burns or Cuts:
Apply lavender neat (undiluted)

Warts:
Apply lemon or tea tree neat (undiluted)

Nervous Tension, Stress, Insomnia:
Roman chamomile, bergamot, sandalwood, lavender, orange

Fatigue, Regaining Strength:
Basil, jasmine, *peppermint,* ylang ylang, neroli, *rosemary*

Caution: *Throughout the text, oils in italics should never be used during pregnancy.*

 Health

CHAPTER 5

The Energy Centers of Your Environment

Chi As the Link

Developing your personal Chi is the most important factor in self-development. The Tree of Life and the Chakra system have given us two ways of viewing how Chi moves through our lives and through our bodies. When Chi is in balance in your body, it is reflected in your life. The same is true with your secondary vessel, your home. When Chi is in balance and harmony in your home, this is mirrored in your life. Good Feng Shui is about making changes in your environment to bring balanced Chi to your home and your life.

> **Your home is the vessel that you have created to hold you, along with the Chi that nurtures your life and livelihood.**

It is easy to see how Chi moves through your body; it is less clear how it moves through a space. But you need only look at Nature to understand its movements. Chi moves through Nature in a smooth and curvilinear pattern, just like a meandering stream. Where Chi moves, it nourishes and gives life to all that it touches. The same holds true for your home. Even though it is a human-made building, Chi still flows through it.

When Chi is moving through your space in a balanced manner, it is able to nurture all that it encounters—including you! If Chi meets a block and is not able to flow smoothly, or if it is pushed and pulled too fast through the space, it cannot impart its life-giving properties. The result is an imbalanced and disharmonious life.

Your home's vital Chi affects all aspects of your life, including your personal Chi and the Chi that moves through your business. Let's see how:

I did a combo-consultation for Lisa on her home and her gift store. Because of the logistics, I did her business before her home. (It is usually better to do it the other way around.) This small store was jammed to capacity, with everything from candy and stuffed animals to high-end bath products and gourmet food. Instead of choosing one theme for her store, she had ten. Instead of having one or two of each specialty gift, she had fifteen or twenty. She was unable to commit to one "specialty" because she was afraid of missing a potential sale.

While Lisa was tying up countless thousands of dollars in inventory (and ordering more while I was there), the customers could hardly move through the store, much less appreciate or find most of the items, as they were packed and stacked in every nook and cranny. There was no Chi moving; there was no space for it to flow. No Chi flow means no customers moving through the store or cash moving through the register. It was clear that Lisa was unable to follow her dream about what kind of specialty store she really wanted, and the store reflected her indecision, fear, and lack of personal Chi.

Since the home always gives away the deeper answer to "what is really going on," I was not at all surprised to find that Lisa's home was just the opposite of her store. It was stark, and devoid of any warm homey touches. It had none of the beautiful specialty items she was selling in her store! Chi was blowing right through her home. It had nothing to slow it down so it could nurture her and her life. Her statement that she wanted a "black and white color scheme" in her home also clearly defined the state of her personal Chi.

But life is not black and white. Chi needs to be flowing smoothly in all aspects of life, not too fast, not too slow, but just right. Lisa's personal Chi was rooted in the extremes. When she made changes in her home to make it more warm and nurturing, it would support her in confronting her personal fears of committing to a specialty store that featured her products properly. Additionally, without her money being tied up in inventory she no longer needed, she would be more relaxed and happy and so would her customers—and happy customers are buying customers!

Listen to what people say. The words that they use tell stories about what is going on inside them. Lisa said that she wanted a "black and white" color scheme in her home. In actuality, her expression was also describing the state of her life at the moment.

Sacred geometry has shown you that a pattern is repeated on both the small scale and the large scale: the microcosm and the macrocosm. Lisa had mirrored in her surroundings the unbalanced Chi that she was feeling in her life. Her store and her home were snapshots of how her life was working.

The solution to unbalanced Chi lies in developing your personal Chi on all levels. The Tree of Life and the Chakra system are two ancient systems of cultivating Chi that can help you manifest balanced Chi in your life. When you have harmony on the inside, it is reflected in your home and your life. But again, go back to the principle of macrocosm/microcosm. Can't it work in the reverse, too? By making changes in your environment, can't you influence changes in your personal Chi? Of course, that *is* the principle of Feng Shui.

The Bagua

Hopefully you now know that Chi is the cohesive force of the cosmos; it is what helps you manifest positive change in your life. Making sure that Chi is flowing harmoniously through your spaces is what good Feng Shui is all about. And just as the Tree of Life and the Chakras give you a specific sacred geometric pattern to follow, so does Feng Shui.

The symbol that Feng Shui experts use to describe the totality of life experience is the Bagua (meaning eight areas). This special octagon is the geometrically defined symbol of the cosmos and the workings of natural laws. It reveals eight specific life energies that serve as guidelines on how to let life blossom to the fullest, and yet allow each and every person to be unique and grow to untold potential.

It is through using the Bagua that you can learn to harmonize your home *and* your life. It helps you chart the essence of life and keep it in balance. The fun part comes when you begin to link your sacred life path as revealed by your personal Bagua with the sacred personalities of the essential oils!

Yin/Yang

The history of the Bagua, which dates back thousands of years, is steeped in fantastic stories of sages and kings and of Heaven and Earth. It is said that this information was received from a celestial source and has guided Asian cultures for thousands of years.

And just as the Kabbalists knew, the ancient Chinese understood that we came from a single source of celestial creation, but on Earth, our physical existence was ruled by an inherent duality. This duality was composed of two opposite yet inseparable elements of universal energy—yang and yin: male and female, light and dark, active and passive, full and empty. These opposing yet interdependent forces of yin and yang permeate our entire existence.

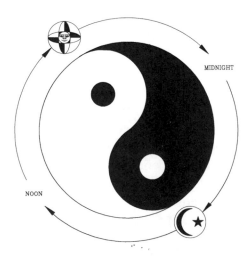

The yin/yang symbol, which became a popular '60s peace icon, also shows that each half of the yin/yang circle contains the seed of the other. In this way, the cycle of life continues; as one ebbs, the other flows; as one dies, the other is born; and as we learned with the Tree of Life, as one imparts, the other receives.

If we look closely at the illustrations on pages 41 and 49, we can see that the polarities of the left and right branches of the Tree of Life are the same as the polarities of yin and yang—and how perfectly human beings fit between them.

Yin contains the essence of yang,
and yang the essence of yin.
Chi perpetuates yin flowing into yang,
and yang into yin.

The Trigrams: The Building Blocks of Life

The graphic representation of yang is a solid line, and yin a broken line. They were combined in a series of three lines of either yin, yang, or a combination of both, for a total of eight trigrams (three lines). These trigrams were primordial symbols through which all phenomena and life could be understood; they were the Chinese archetypal symbols to describe our existence.

Keep in mind that the Chinese culture was very lyrical and pictorial. They spoke and wrote of their advanced scientific and mathematical knowledge not only in symbols, as we in the West do, but in terms of Nature and the endless flow of Chi. Their scientific language was profound and poetic because they believed that the force and beauty of Mother Nature was inherent in all disciplines.

The trigrams, which symbolized the basic building blocks of life, were associated with eight basic energies. They were given names from Nature that mirrored the energy being described: Heaven, Earth, Water, Fire, Lake, Mountain, Thunder, and Wind. Each represented an area of life, a specific life energy—different from the rest, but necessary for the whole. Each side of the Bagua corresponds to one of the eight types of life Chi. Taken as a whole, it can be seen as a type of life map. This symbol, the eight life energies arranged in an octagon, was how the Chinese viewed the manifest universe; that is, our physical environment.

Water = Career and Life Journey

Mountain = Self-Cultivation/Knowledge

Thunder = Family and Health

Wind = Wealth

Fire = Fame and Recognition

Earth = Marriage and Partnership

Lake = Children and Creativity

Heaven = Helpful People and Travel

These are very visual correspondences. When you think of self-cultivation, perhaps a person in lotus position meditating comes to mind. Doesn't that image remind you of a still mountain? What about a solid, loving partnership? Doesn't that feel like the stable and bountiful Earth beneath you? And your life journey—can't you visualize it as a river of water flowing gently to the sea?

Three Systems, One Answer

The Bagua is a pattern of understanding how Chi manifests and moves through our homes. The Chakra system shows how it moves and manifests in our bodies, and the Tree of Life reveals Chi's workings in the cosmos. It seems straightforward, doesn't it? Each system explains a separate area of our lives, right? Wrong!

**Each contains the essence of how to cultivate
Chi flow in our lives and homes.**

The Bagua, the Chakras, and the Tree of Life all use sacred geometric layouts to help reveal the mysteries of being human. When we combine these transcendental patterns, we see that they are similar in the path that they take us on.

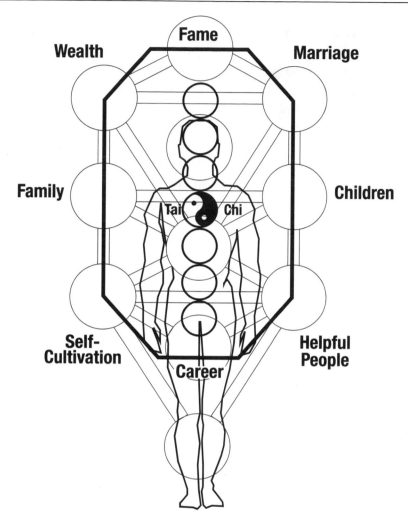

Fame

Wealth

Marriage

Family

Tai Chi

Children

Self-
Cultivation

Career

Helpful
People

If you overlay the Bagua on top of the Tree of Life,[20] you can see that the middle pillar or trunk of the tree aligns with the center of the Bagua as well as with the Chakras. The *Career Gua*[21] of the Bagua— your life path and career—coincides with the *Foundation* of the Tree of Life. These in turn correspond to the *Root Chakra,* your grounding mechanism in life. All three systems speak of the same concept, the same energy that must be present in your life in order to have a solid base on which to build: grounding and foundation. If you do not have a

---

[20] Review the correspondences of the Chakras and the Tree of Life, page 49.
[21] Gua is one section of the eight-sectioned Ba-Gua. The term *Gua* will be interchangeable with the term *area* or *energy center*.

solid base on Earth, all that you try to develop or build on top of it will come crashing down.

The center of the Bagua, which is the center of the home, is called the *Tai Chi*. With its central support system of *Family/Health* on one side and *Children/Creativity* on the other, it corresponds to *Beauty* at the heart center of the Tree of Life. In the Chakra system, you learned that the heart Chakra is the center of your body's energetic system. And it is from this central location that love expands out to the rest of the Chakras. Isn't this how it operates in your home as well? When health and love radiate out from you to your family and children, it also nourishes the rest of your life.

Each of these heart centers speaks of the transformative power of love.

Your material existence is necessary for you to survive and learn all that you need to as a human. But if you do not progress through the experience of love and transform the more material aspects of yourself into the more spiritual ones, you will never be able to attune to your higher self. These are the energy centers of transformation.

As the plug into the universal energy, you have seen that the *Crown sephiroth* and the *Crown Chakra* perform similar functions. This is the center through which you are able to connect to your own Divine essence. In the Bagua, the *Fame Gua* is the center through which you reach the higher expression of who you are. Following your Divine bliss, you will easily be recognized in sharing your higher expressive self.

In exploring the information from any of these systems or all of them combined, you can delve deeper into yourself to understand your own internal mechanisms. When you are able to understand what you are made of, you can begin to mold who you are and where you are going. The old adage, "Knowledge is power," is certainly true. When you discover all these energy or power centers that make up you, your space, and your cosmos, you can use them to become a Creator and to *receive* the kind of life that you were meant to live.

The fact that the Bagua, the Tree of Life, and the Chakra system are still valid and accessible tools thousands of years after they were first practiced is a living testament to the ancients' understanding of how Nature's laws applied to human beings.

**The root of all these disciplines is the same.
Each leads us on a path of self-exploration
and spiritual development.**

It also shows that each of these viewpoints, while growing from the same roots, has different flowers blooming on its branches—each fragrant, each lovely in its own right. And, having this variety of philosophical blossoms and scents in your garden only makes it richer and more beautiful.

Using the Bagua

In order to better understand your path, you need to look deeper into the Bagua so you can come to know what your space is trying to tell you about your life. The Bagua becomes a working tool that you can use to identify, raise, and change the Chi in any space, whether that be your home, office, yard, or bedroom. When you make a change or adjustment in your home, represented by a specific area in the Bagua, you bring positive changes to that specific area of your life, too.

The Bagua is overlaid onto your floor plan and is oriented by the location of the entrance. The Career Gua is always positioned along the wall where the main door, or mouth of Chi, is located. The Bagua is elongated or shortened to fit the size of the area. The Bagua can be used over the entire home, yard, office building, or space. It can also be used over each individual room or area; it is oriented the same way, with the career area positioned along the wall where the entrance of the room is.

The Bagua is a flexible tool that can be used on many different levels. You can use it:

- on the macro/macro level—over your entire home
  site, which would include the yard and the land the
  house (office, apartment complex, etc.) is built on.

81

- on the macro level—over the entire house (using the architectural floor plan is helpful).

- on the micro level—each specific room has its own Bagua.

- on the micro/micro level—each piece of furniture can be used with a Bagua overlay.

If the space is irregularly shaped or missing a corner, it may mean imbalances in the corresponding life energy. In other words, if one area is missing, your home and perhaps your life is out of sync because that part of the whole is out of balance. It is possible to change imbalanced for missing areas and overall out-of-syncness by working with the Bagua.[22]

Front of House or Any Room

Exercise:

The way that you decorate and set up your home tells stories about what is happening in your life. By looking at your space through "fresh eyes," as if you were walking into it for the first time, you can learn how to recognize imbalances in your life. It will also help you to get started on the proper Feng Shui changes. Let's explore the areas of the Bagua and get to know what the Chi of each area is about.

ℰ   ℰ   ℰ

A good exercise is to use your "fresh eyes" and physically go to

---

[22] For more information, see the Feng Shui solutions to Maryann and Steve's problems in chapter 8, and *Feng Shui Today: Earth Design the Added Dimension*.

each area of your home while you read and contemplate the meaning of the Gua. Jot down your initial impressions of the space. Do you feel happy here? Is it one of your favorite parts in your home? Do you avoid coming here? Is it dark? Airy? Dirty? Well kept? Is it filled with things you love? What does it smell like? Dank? Fresh? Fragrantly yummy? Does it feel harmonious or somehow out of sync?

Most times you can feel when your space is off-balance. For some reason you feel uncomfortable, not quite at home in your own home. Or, there are certain rooms that you or your guests just do not like to spend time in. These are indications that Chi is not flowing properly. You might shrug off the idea, especially if the room that you feel uncomfortable in is the guest bedroom. "What does it matter?" you ask. "I never really use that room anyway." It matters a lot! If part of your space is out of sync, it means that a part of the whole is out of balance.

Use the questions after each area to ask yourself: *Is this area of my home and life in balance? Does it need work? Is everything in great shape? Am I ready for a change?* Try not to think too much about the answers.

**Just let them flow from how you feel,
not what you think the answers should be.**

After concentrating on the issues of the Bagua, try making a link with the Chakras and the Chi that each represents. For example, the career area of the Bagua is about your life's path, and the root Chakra resonates with the energy of survival, or meeting your financial needs of being grounded. Both, in fact, speak of the *foundation* in your life. There is similar energy between the two.

This knowledge can help you make simultaneous Chi-enhancing changes in your home and your body. Fragrant Feng Shui relates to personal Chi issues that are also visible in the body through the Chakras. Working with the Bagua energy centers and the body energy centers in tandem, you can resolve personal issues, and you can get on with your life free of baggage.

**All personal issues that are uncovered by
Feng Shui also connect to the Chakras.**

However, we must not become too rigid in making our correspondences. While the sacred geometry of the Bagua and the Chakras do
work together, they are not the same and can mean different things at
different times in our lives.

The Career Area

This is the energy center of your
career as well as your life path. Your
job is an important component of your
life—you spend half of your waking
hours doing it. Does it jibe with your
goals for what kind of life you would
like to live? (Remember the new goals
that you set in chapter 2.)

- Do you spend your work and free time engaged in
  similar pursuits?
- Does your career truly reflect the kind of person you
  are on the inside?
- Do you really like your work and truly enjoy *going*
  to work?
- Does your work bring joy to you, your family, those
  who are in your industry, and those who use your
  products, services, or talents?
- Is your work or workplace environmentally friendly?

We know that the Root Chakra corresponds with the Career Gua.
Both speak of your life path and being rooted in Mother Earth. If
you are not stable in your finances and your sense of self in the
world as the Root Chakra teaches, how can you know what your life
path is? Depending on the point in life where you are, this information may mean different things. In college, survival means having
enough to pay the rent, buy books, and a pitcher of beer on the

weekends. Your life path at the time is clear: *Make it through exams*. As you hit the real world, your life path and survival issues change. Survival may mean supporting children or aging parents; your life path may mean finding a job you love instead of one that just pays well. As you retire, perhaps the path leads you to becoming the best senior golfer at the club or the spokesperson for an environmental group.

Essential Oils for the Career Gua and Root Chakra[23]

Black pepper: Fosters security, endurance, protection, physical energy, courage, stamina, motivation, changeability. Helps to counteract fatigue, confusion, indecision, irrationality, frustration, mental exhaustion.

Cinnamon: Fosters strength, practicality, steadfastness, physical energy, prosperity. Helps to counteract instability, exhaustion.

Ginger: Fosters courage, physical energy, encouragement, fortitude. Helps to counteract lack of direction, purposelessness, lack of focus, fatigue, burnout, apathy.

Patchouli: Fosters physical energy, money, assuredness, vigor, stimulation. Helps to counteract indecision, sluggishness, tension, mood swings, stress.

Vetiver: Fosters grounding, centering, strength, protection, money, integrity, mind-body connection, honor, self-esteem. Helps to counteract fear, overwork, intellectual fatigue, irritability, burnout, exhaustion, loss of purpose.

Caution: *Throughout the text, oils in italics should never be used during pregnancy.*

---

[23] Since all oils have many life-enhancing attributes, the oils listed for each Gua and Chakra are not exhaustive.

The Self-Cultivation/ Knowledge Area

Moving clockwise around the Bagua wheel, we move into the Self-Cultivation area. This is the Gua that speaks of who you are on the inside. Many times the person on the inside is not the same one that shows its face on the outside. Because we are in a very important, transformational time, it is becoming mandatory that we start living as we are meant to; we need to follow our bliss. This area deals with your ability to pursue your personal, spiritual path as well as any studies or educational work.

- Do you have one face at work, another at home, and another with family members?
- Do you have a personal, spiritual component to your life? (This doesn't mean just attending a church or following a religious doctrine.)
- Is there something you have always wanted to study or learn, but have never gotten around to it?
- Do you have an area in your house that is dedicated to your spiritual side? A small altar? A special chair where you are silent or meditative?
- Do you share your insights with the rest of your family?

Which Chakra speaks to you of knowledge, of self-development, of seeing and understanding? Isn't the Third-Eye Chakra the center from which you gain insight from the world around you? When you are open to the intuitive flow of knowledge that comes through this psychic center, then you begin to gain valuable insight into who you really are and where you really want to be headed on your life path.

Feng Shui is a catalyst for healing because it *calls people on their stuff*. It is a mirror that makes you take a deeper look into the issues in your life. It reveals subconscious information that can help you make changes. Where you have subconsciously placed an accessory and what that accessory symbolizes may be an indication of something you need to look at concerning your personal issues.

Lisette called me to help mend her broken heart. Her fiancé had just moved out; it was the latest in a string of severed relationships. At 41, what she most wanted in her life was to be married (she had never been) and to have a child. Intuitively (Third-Eye Chakra was working), she had gone out and purchased a kissing couple sculpture that she absolutely loved. While dusting, it fell and the man's head broke off. In her "Oh my goodness, I'll never get married" fear, she promptly got out the glue.

What does this situation say to you? Automatically you might think that this relates to the Sex Chakra/Marriage Gua, but that is not entirely true. Close your eyes, use your Third Eye, and ask your higher self what this situation is truly about!

It's about self-cultivation. The accessory was speaking to Lisette, telling her that she really wasn't ready to find a new relationship because it would just break again. She had never stopped to question what she may have been doing to sabotage her relationships. It was clear to me, because there was "separation in the sculpture," that the timing was not right for her to set the energy in motion for a new relationship. There was some other resolution necessary first. What the universe and her subconscious energy were suggesting is that she needed to know herself and to stand in her own power first. By doing this, she would know what would really make her happy in a relationship, instead of settling for something that, in her desperation, was doomed to fail or would ultimately create unhappiness.

This is an underrated Gua. While all the Guas and life situations affect and influence all the others, this one relates to personal Chi like no other. And hopefully by now, you know that it is foremost in your life and Feng Shui.

Pay attention to the nuances of space and accessories—this is Feng Shui!

Essential Oils for the Self-Cultivation Gua and Third-Eye Chakra

Basil: Fosters the conscious mind, awakening, clarity, stimulation, purposefulness, trust, strength, enthusiasm, cheerfulness. Helps to counteract mental fatigue and exhaustion, lack of focus and direction, burnout, confusion, indecision.

Eucalyptus: Fosters alertness, concentration, stimulation, emotional and energy balance, logical thought, positive change, freedom. Helps to counteract irrational thought, explosive argumentativeness, lack of concentration, mood swings.

Juniper: Fosters alertness, focus, sacredness, vision, spiritual support, enlightenment, meditation, wisdom, humility. Helps to counteract nervous and mental exhaustion, lack of self-worth, dissatisfaction, guilt.

Lemon: Fosters concentration, focus, purification, clarity, awareness, consciousness. Helps to counteract mental blocks and fatigue, resentfulness, depression, apathy, humorlessness, stress, fear, irritability.

Peppermint: Fosters the conscious mind, alertness, concentration, regeneration, refreshment, vitality. Helps to counteract mental fatigue, sluggishness, lethargy, apathy, helplessness.

Rosemary: Fosters the conscious mind, memory, concentration, regeneration, centering, clarity. Helps to counteract loss of memory, learning difficulties, disorientation, indecision, strain, emotional exhaustion.

Caution: *Throughout the text, oils in italics should never be used during pregnancy.*

The Family Area

Follow the universal wheel. Start seeing it in your mind's eye so you can always carry it with you.

This Gua is about your family, which may be your birth family or may extend to include your close friends who support and love you like family. This area is related to your ancestors—those who have gone before you and paved the way for who you are, and who you can become. It also extends to the larger community. Feng Shui is about realizing that we are all connected. We are truly a world team, and we have to start playing together and loving one another.

- Are you on good terms with your siblings and parents? Until there is harmony at home, we can never hope to have harmony in the world.
- Is your family life at home good?
- Do you have heart-to-heart talks with your children at family dinners?
- Do you speak with, send prayers to, or honor your grandparents in some way (both those living and those who have passed away)?
- Do you volunteer your time to your community or give donations to charities that support positive change in the world?

The family is the center from which you emerged into adulthood. Which Chakra resonates with the feeling of being centered among loved ones? The Heart Chakra, of course. From here springs all the love that you need to get by. Family—genetic, adopted, chosen friends—these are all sources of the unconditional love we need to experience along our life path.

This center Chakra is associated with the center of our home.

Family is our support system, the best experience we have of unconditional love. Who has not witnessed this bond in the energy spiraling out from a mother to her newborn? Our families are also good lessons in love; they are our karmic lesson of unconditional love. We did not choose them, at least not consciously, and yet our parents gave us the gift of life. We can learn true unconditional love when we learn to accept our siblings and parents *exactly* as they are. They are merely mirrors for our souls.[24]

The Wealth Area

I know what you're thinking: *Wealth! I definitely want more money. My life would be perfect if only I had "X" more dollars.* But wealth is a lot more than material riches, which, don't get me wrong, are also important in laying a stable foundation in our lives. Wealth is also about wealth of spirit, of friendship, and of relationship. It is about giving and receiving in equal portions.

- Do you have enough money so that you are financially fit? (Remember, there is a difference between being fit and being secure—even Ted Turner has admitted that he is not "secure" with his fortune...seems a bit out of balance, but then again, aren't we all human, with the same life concerns?)
- Are you generous with your wealth—whether that be money, time, love, or your talents?
- Do you give as much as you receive?
- Do you judge people by how much money they have or by the good works that they do?
- Are you quick to share?

---

[24] Please refer to the essential oils for the Heart Chakra (see page 62) and the Tai Chi/Health Gua (see page 102).

Abundance, wealth, power—these are all the domain of the third Chakra, the seat of will. With the power of will, you can draw to you all the abundance that the earth has to offer. But will works in many aspects of your life. In order to change to a better job, you need will; to hang on in a worthy relationship that is going through rough times, you need will. It also comes full circle. By using will to help you accomplish these goals, you can gain the abundance of wealth (spiritual and economic) from your new job, and the abundance of love from a relationship that is good for you.

Essential Oils for the Wealth Gua and Will Chakra

Bergamot: Fosters confidence, assertiveness, creativity, performance, encouragement, strength, motivation, completeness. Helps to counteract helplessness, burnout, exhaustion, stress, tension.

Atlas cedarwood: Fosters assertiveness, confidence, self-image, self-control, dignity, power, persistence, fortitude, nobility of spirit. Helps to counteract overanalysis, selfishness, worry, fear, scattered thoughts, anxiety.

Cypress: Fosters assertiveness, confidence, creativity, self-image, wisdom, direction, righteousness, strength, courage, generosity, power, straightforwardness. Helps to counteract fear, the inability to speak up for oneself, being overly opinionated, uncontrolled passions.

Frankincense: Fosters the self-image, assertiveness, performance, positivity, acceptance, resolution, fortitude. Helps to counteract fears, burnout, overattachments, exhaustion, self-destruction, apprehension.

Ginger: Fosters strength, confidence, assertiveness, courage, warmth, fortitude, empathy. Helps to counteract lack of direction, purposelessness, loss of focus, apathy, burnout, fatigue.

Caution: *Throughout the text, oils in italics should never be used during pregnancy.*

91

The Fame Area

The Fame Gua is about being recognized for who you are and what you do. There is no one else in the world who was born into the same time and conditions as you were, so you are in a unique position to give the world something that no one else can.[25] When you tap into this essence, you are able to blossom in a unique way. How do you want to be seen in the world? Are you wise, funny, intelligent, warm, serious...? Fame is about truly expressing who you are. Let the world know about YOU!

- Do you cultivate your special talents, or are you still hiding them under a bushel?
- Are you afraid to speak about yourself in front of a crowd?
- Do you take credit where credit is due?
- Is the image you project to the world the person you feel you are on the inside?
- Are you able to stand up for yourself?

Your unique place in the world—being seen for who you really are—is about connecting to your higher self, your true self. Which Chakra plugs you into this Divine source? The Crown Chakra is your electrical outlet into the cosmos. It allows you to tap into your essence and then show it to the world.

> *Fran, a very gifted psychic and healer, with a very open Crown Chakra, asked me to Feng Shui her home. She wanted to make shifts for more professional recognition, which would enhance her career and income. When I walked through her home, her most important Fame areas had problems. (Notice how all the energy centers in your*

---

[25] Remember the tenet of the Kabbalah: *To receive, you must also share*. Native North Americans call this same concept a "giveaway."

home work together creating the whole, the same way that all the Chakras define your entire being.)

The Fame area of the living room, the room of first impression,[26] had a distorted mirror on the Fame wall. When clients came for readings, they had to pass through the living room and were greeted by a distorted vision of themselves. In the Fame area of Fran's home, the room where she did her readings, all the Chi of recognition was going right through these sliding glass doors and was watered down in the pool outside.

While the clients received clear and true information from this talented lady, it may have been distorted by the client's own misinterpretation after just having experienced the distortion of the mirror. Once in the reading room, the room facing the pool, memories of the experience might have been diluted. All these negatives greeted both Fran and the client; the issue of fame, of being recognized in her profession, was being diluted and distorted.

Remember the concept of the macro/micro for the Bagua: For example, there is a Fame area of the entire house, plus a Fame area of each individual room. Many times an issue, in Fran's case that of Fame, is repeated in both the macro and the micro.

Fran had a distorted mirror in the Fame area of her living room (micro); she also had one in the "watered-down" Fame area of her entire house (macro). Look around your house to see if an issue is being repeated on the micro and macro.

Take a look at how the Feng Shui of an environment affects the Chakra/Bagua relationship, along with life situations. Look around your home. What is there that may be influencing you?

---

[26] The room of first impression is the room you see when you first enter a space. It is vital to your Feng Shui experience, since it shifts your energy from the external world to the internal. Seeing positive or negative Feng Shui every time you enter your sacred space makes a lasting impression.

Essential Oils for the Fame Gua and Crown Chakra

Clary sage: Fosters euphoria, calmness, dreams, self-awareness, warmth, harmony, balance, tranquility, inspiration. Helps to counteract delusion, burnout, emotional debility, melancholy, depression, nightmares, nervousness, tension, stress.

Frankincense: Fosters spirituality, meditation, wisdom, healing, emotional stability, enlightenment, introspection, inspiration. Helps to counteract overattachments, blockages, grief, burnout, self-destruction, despair, resistance, exhaustion, fear, disconnection, repression.

Jasmine (E): Fosters spirituality, psychic dreams, self-awareness, euphoria, intuition, profoundness, awareness, joy. Helps to counteract pessimism, indifference, jealousy, bitterness, emotional frigidity and abuse, low self-esteem, depression, anxiety.

Roman chamomile (E): Fosters meditation, peacefulness, healing, understanding, empathy, patience, stillness, relaxation, awareness/recognition of spirit. Helps to counteract moroseness, deep emotional baggage, spiritual disconnection, worry, stress, anger, depression.

Sandalwood: Fosters self-awareness, spirituality, meditation, enlightenment, balance, connection, unity, comfort, insight, harmony, serenity. Helps to counteract possessiveness, inability to forgive, manipulation, cynicism, aggression, distress, insecurity, anxiety, nervous tension, irritability, obsessiveness.

(E): These oils are either rare or require more plant material to make the oil; thus, they are considerably more expensive.

Caution: *Throughout the text, oils in italics should never be used during pregnancy.*

The Marriage/Relationship Area

Partnership has become a focal point in our society. Pop psychology books abound with advice on how to find the perfect mate, but marriage and relationships are much more than that. First we need to have a good relationship with ourselves (linked to the Self-Cultivation area) before we can look to share it with others. Remember Lisette's story (page 87)? A marriage or relationship means much more than romance-novel adventures and sex. Equally important is how to nurture a relationship through the down cycles or hard times (and there are always going to be down cycles—it is the nature of our world), and celebrate the up cycles or good times.

- Before you try to find a partner or *fix* the one you have, ask if you have done groundwork on yourself first.

- Do you put your partner before yourself?

- Do you expect more from your partner than you are willing to give?

- Are there equal parts romance, fun, talking, listening, loving, and alone time in your relationship?

- Are you in a relationship (or do you find yourself in a continual string of relationships) that does not let you fully express who you are?

- Are you in a solid, loving relationship? This, too, must be watered and fertilized in order to keep it growing!

The correspondence between this area of the Bagua and the Sex Chakra looks straightforward, but life is never so simple, is it? Relationships are much more complex than just sex. They include business partnerships, family relationships, and friendships. Each of these relationships must also find its power in the second Chakra. Every relationship must also move up to be transformed by the Heart Chakra and, if possible, all be brought into the realm of oneness through the Crown Chakra.

When you look at the issues that relate to the Chakras/Guas, remember that they can be pertinent on many levels, not just the most obvious. Ask yourself, **What does this mean to me?**

Essential Oils for the Marriage Gua and Sex Chakra

Geranium: Fosters creativity, comfort, balance, humor, security. Helps to counteract fear, extreme moods, insecurity, lack of self-esteem, being overly emotional, sensitivity.

Grapefruit: Fosters emotional clarity, vigor, refreshment, joy, confidence, positivity, spontaneity, emotional purification. Helps to counteract dependency, self-doubt, self-criticism.

Orange: Fosters purification, joy, physical energy, contentment, happiness, self-image.

Pine: Fosters self-forgiveness, acceptance, physical energy, understanding, forgiving, sharing, trusting, acceptance of love. Helps to counteract regret, guilt, dissatisfaction, self-criticism, being nonconfrontational, unworthiness, being unsympathetic, feeling inadequate.

Sandalwood: Fosters contentment, joy, restfulness, self-awareness, self-esteem, self-image, sex, creativity.

Ylang ylang: Fosters sexuality, sensuousness, positive emotions, unity, joy, self-confidence, warmth. Helps to counteract resentment, jealousy, selfishness, stubbornness, obstinacy, shyness.

The Children/ Creativity Area

Children are the result of pro-*creation*. This area is as much about your children as it is about your creativity. You must nurture your creative side just as you do your children. Without love and care, children do not blossom into their fullness, nor will your life be an ongoing, creative event unless you pay attention to it and care for it.

- If you have children, do you make enough time each day to help them grow? (Remember how tough it was just to grow up.)

- If you are considering having children, are you willing to give up your current life for this new journey? In my opinion, children should never be second to a career or any other pursuit.

- Do you have hobbies that you enjoy?

- Do you bring creativity into your everyday life?

- When was the last time you constructed, painted, molded, wrote, designed, refinished, revamped, sang, danced...?

- Do your work (Career Gua) and your relationship (Marriage/Relationship Gua) lives foster your creativity or hinder it?

Children are part of the heart center of your home and life. Creativity also stems from this area of the Bagua. Creativity is not just painting a great picture; it is also about solving problems in new ways. It is about searching for avenues to express your uniqueness—whether that be creating exotic meals for your family, making chairs from recycled materials, or developing creativity in your career. It is anything that comes from the heart that expresses who you are. This creativity is also nurtured by being connected through the Root and Crown Chakras into our dual sources of Chi—the earth and the cosmos.[27]

The Helpful People/Travel Area

This Gua tends to be the least understood and probably the most neglected. But as we have seen with our sacred geometry, wholeness counts. Without this Gua, we would be lacking. Who are the helpful people in your life? Consider anybody who enriches your life and makes it run more smoothly: your doctor, baby-sitter, teacher, mechanic, mentor, UPS man, pastor...the list is endless, and each person's help is indispensable.

We need each other!

This Gua also has to do with travel and movement.

- Are you aware of the circle of helpful people that you have around you?

- Do you have problems with doctors canceling appointments, baby-sitters not showing up, promised deliveries arriving late, and the like?

- Do you offer your time and talents to help others out—to be a mentor to a small child, to carpool, to coach a little league sport, to take your grand-mother to the doctor...?

- If your dream is to travel, have you been able to go to the places that you have always dreamed of visiting?

---

[27] Please refer to the essential oils for the Heart Chakra (see page 62) and the Tai Chi/Health Gua (see page 102).

The Helpful People area speaks of your relations with the people you come in contact with. Each person you deal with is both a source of support and a means through which you can learn. When you start to interact on a free and truthful level with everyone, you begin living a path of truth. Which Chakra is about speaking and living your truth? The Throat Chakra. Speaking your true feelings means living exactly as you were meant to. When you are living in perfect harmony with your higher self, it is of benefit to everyone.

As I entered John and Judith's home, my throat constricted and I started to cough. Interesting, isn't it? The house was full of clutter and was musty-dusty-awful. They had so much disorganized stuff that I couldn't even get into some of the rooms.

They were both working on some pretty weighty body, mind, and spirit issues. John was receiving chemotherapy for cancer. And as children, both had been sexually abused. (Talk about some heavy karma they were living jointly.)

Over the past several years, Judith had processed her trauma and was able to speak its truth, unclogging her Throat Chakra. John, on the other hand, had been brought up to never speak about "private issues," so he had never dealt with the impact of what had happened to him. (Again, we see the importance of the Self-Cultivation Gua; see how it keeps reoccurring?) The cancer John was suffering from was throat cancer. Does it surprise you? By never speaking his truth, he had shut down the proper function of the energies of the Throat Chakra. Blocked Chakras mean disease.

I asked him why he didn't begin his emotional healing and start speaking his truth. He replied, "I watched my wife go through such pain; I just can't do it." Instead, he "chose" throat cancer as his way to process. Karmic energy generated from positive or negative experiences, in this life or previous lives, must manifest in some way. Does it surprise you that the room where he shook off the poison from his chemotherapy was in the Helpful People area, and that he wasn't letting anyone help him with the real issue?

While sitting in his favorite chair, which faced an industrial-sized hospital clock, John made his choice as he watched his time tick away....

A cluttered home means a cluttered life. How can you even begin to work on yourself if you can't move past the old and outdated, literally and figuratively? Clutter is one of the biggest Feng Shui no-no's. It means you are hanging on to things you don't really need anymore. If there is a pile somewhere, chances are 100 to 1 that you do not even know what is at the bottom! If it is not serving you, get rid of it. My two favorite Feng Shui words: no mercy!

Essential Oils for the Helpful People/Travel Gua and Throat Chakra

Lavender: Fosters assistance, acceptance, integrity, directness, compassion, security, relaxation, alertness, emotional balance. Helps to counteract insecurity, moodiness, agitation, burnout, jitteriness, conflict, obsessive behavior.

Lemon: Fosters communication, acceptance, directness, versatility, stimulation, emotional and mental clarity, direction, calmness, liveliness. Helps to counteract distrust, resentment, indecision, irritability, bad attitudes.

Peppermint: Fosters decisiveness, communication, acceptance, penetration, vitality, vibrance. Helps to counteract mood swings, indecision, tension, stress, anxiety, depression, selfishness, touchiness.

Pine: Fosters forgiveness, directness, acceptance, understanding, patience, humility, sharing, mindfulness, trust, acceptance of help. Helps to counteract dissatisfaction, worry, feeling overly responsible for others.

Thyme: Fosters decisiveness, conviction, gentle empowerment, vigor, tolerance, support, warmth. Helps to counteract lack of direction, intellectual and physical exhaustion, overreactions, blockages.

Caution: *Throughout the text, oils in italics should never be used during pregnancy.*

The Tai Chi or Center

This is the area that combines the other eight energies. The center of your space reflects the wholeness of your experience. In Feng Shui it is also related to health. Remember that health is really about being whole—all your physical systems are functioning well, and you feel good in body, mind, and spirit. The Tai Chi also relates to creativity. When you are able to integrate all of your talents from each of the areas of your life, you can create anything you want.

- Do you feel whole? Or does it feel that parts of your life just don't mesh with other aspects?
- Are you in good health—emotionally, physically, and spiritually?
- Do you feel as if your life is in balance?
- What, if anything, is missing from your life?
- Are you using your creative talents?

The center of the home is the heart center of the body's Chakras and of the cosmos, as the Kabbalah has shown us. When love spirals from your heart center, it bathes the rest of your life in positive energy, making all the pieces fit together better.

When I started writing this book, I started getting pains in my chest, my heart center, while relaxing at night, readying for dream-time. Oh, no, here we go! I thought, What's up?

I know all too well about these self-inflicted stress indicators caused by self-imposed deadlines. I am a classic type-A personality and demand a lot from myself even though I love my work. I am out of town sometimes for months at a time and am home only for a brief catch-up, which is never quite the same as catching your breath.

After six months of being on the road, I had cleared my schedule for several months of spiritual, regenerative time that would also be the perfect time to write this book. This is all higher-minded cultivation, the energies depicted on the "top half" of the Tree of Life, and the three "upper" Chakras. Additionally, now that I was home and not dependant on restaurant food, I could get back into my dance class and better eating habits. I was really focused on getting the energies (and abs, butt, and thighs!), the "bottom half" of the Tree of Life, and the three "lower" Chakras, into prime shape.

But due to self-imposed pressure, the book wasn't flowing, I was exercising but still not eating as I should, and worst of all, my husband and I were just barely getting along. Assessing my situation, I realized that I was concentrating so hard on the "uppers" and "lowers" that I forgot to make the heart connection to unify the higher-mindedness with grounded, earthbound energy. I was pushing so hard on either end, I forgot to love the evolutionary experience of writing and the joy of honoring my body. I forgot to love the one who gives me the most love and support. Without my heart in it, my two halves were split. My spiritual mind was disconnected from my body, and my heart was literally aching, reminding me to lighten up and love—love everything!

As soon as I recognized how I was limiting my life experience, I opened up my heart, and, duh, guess what? Immediately, the book started to flow (and it was enlightening and fun), my diet became more regular, my relationship shifted back to the heart, and my chest pains stopped.

Essential Oils for the Tai Chi/Health, Family, and Children Guas, along with the Heart Chakra

Clove: Fosters healing, contentment, creativity, happiness, protection. Helps to counteract anger, misery, worthlessness.

Lavender: Fosters health, love, inner peace, contentment, rest, care, compassion, gentleness, balance, comfort. Helps to counteract anxiety, stress, tension, fear, insecurity, addictions, worry, burnout, conflict.

Orange: Fosters contentment, happiness, joy, warmth, sunny feelings, balance, lightheartedness. Helps to counteract depression, helplessness, sadness, feelings of withdrawal, heavy-heartedness, emotional abuse, worry, obsessions, addictions, anxiety.

Pine: Fosters understanding, patience, acceptance, healing, forgiveness, self-forgiveness, sharing, trust, acceptance of love, exhilaration. Helps to counteract regret, self-blame, dissatisfaction, unworthiness, exhaustion, shame, rejection, inadequacy.

Rose (E): Fosters love, peace, sex, beauty, comfort, reassurance, harmony, passion, cooperation, fulfillment, forgiveness. Helps to counteract bitterness, sadness, fear of letting go, fear of love, fear of not being loved, jealousy, self-destruction, broken hearts, emotional hurts, and abuse.

Roman chamomile (E): Fosters peace, joy, healing, relaxation, understanding, empathy, calmness. Helps to counteract tension, nerves, frustration, emotional dramas, resentment, deep emotional baggage, indifference.

Sandalwood: Fosters contentment, joy, restfulness, healing, balance, warmth, unity, comfort, trust, openness. Helps to counteract anxiety, tension, possessiveness, manipulation, the inability to forgive, lack of acceptance, selfishness, aggressiveness.

Ylang ylang: Fosters peace, love, joy, contentment, unification, warmth, enthusiasm. Helps to counteract depression, tension, stress, frustration, emotional guilt, jealousy, selfishness, resentment, impatience, shyness.

(E): These oils are either rare or require more plant material to make the oil; thus, they are considerably more expensive.

Caution: *Oils in italics should never be used during pregnancy.*

How Does All of This Apply to Your Home?

When you examine the different areas in your life and home, you usually find corresponding areas of harmony or imbalance. For example, if your career is on the rocks—you are unhappy with your boss, you haven't gotten a raise in four years, and the 80-hour work weeks have taken a toll on your family—the Career Gua is probably the area of your house where there are major problems.

A problem on the physical level in your home mirrors a similar imbalance on the psychological or spiritual level.

It might be that in the area of your house that corresponds to the Career Gua, there are mechanical problems that are the physical manifestation of the issues you are experiencing in your life. For example, a water pipe might be leaking and spreading a stain on the ceiling, as in one of my scariest Feng Shui experiences:

> *I walked into the entryway of Rose's home, the room of first impressions, and saw that the ceiling had a large stain and was bubbled out. Rose told me not to worry about it (a huge problem on the ceiling of the Career area of her home!), and in the same breath she explained that there was no room for advancement in her career, but she was still a workaholic and allowed people to take advantage of her.*
>
> *These were clearly Career issues that were literally hanging over her head. But they also were issues of Self-Cultivation, as she was very insecure about career moves; and of Wealth, as she was worried about finances if she did change jobs. All of this was giving her stress headaches (again, the problem was literally hanging over her head).*

 Look at your literal and symbolic relationships. What are you subconsciously trying to tell yourself through your home?

> *Minutes later, while in another room, I thought I heard the sound of water coming from the entry. As we reached the sound, we saw that the bubble had turned into a gigantic watermelon, and water was flooding the entire living room. "Chicken Little, the sky is falling!" I was there to witness Rose's career and possibly her life come crashing in on her. Rose had no choice but to regain self-cultivated confidence to make career choices in order to literally keep her roof from caving in on her.*
>
> *Was it synchronicity that I was there at the same time the problem reached critical mass? Interestingly enough, Rose had rescheduled our appointment three times. According to the natural law that*

"there are no coincidences," the time was ripe for us to experience this disaster together to help Rose see the urgency and clarity that something must "give" in her life or she was going to be physically and emotionally sick.

In this situation, it would be good (imperative) Feng Shui to fix the problem as soon as possible. Even better would be to not let a situation like that get out of hand: "A stitch in time saves nine." Don't let your life hit the skids—clearing up problems that exist is one way to alleviate disharmony. But, Feng Shui is not just about relating leaks and broken doors to problems in your life. It is also about being proactive.

Perhaps your career is fine and you certainly don't have catastrophic leaks, but if it doesn't really *mean* much to you, it is just a job. We are living in critical times, where each step we take has an impact on the globe—whether we focus on the environment or other humans. We cannot live just to get by. We must shape our world. Do not waste your precious time or energy in the pursuit of something that just helps you get by.

Start living life like it really matters to you and the planet.

Feng Shui is about taking proactive steps to enhance your life. We are going to explore ways that you can take charge of your life and set it on a course that will do just that. This means integrating all your *self-knowledge*, your personal Chi, and using it to make not only yourself happier and healthier, but the planet as well.

Take a deep breath, and know that we have gotten over the hard part. Also, know that none of this self-exploration has to be dull or difficult. In fact, this book is a manual about making life changes fun. We are going to use fragrance and some Feng Shui common sense to make your life happier, more joyful, and definitely better smelling!

PART II

Good
Scents

Good Scents

Camping:

Bring your lavender, geranium, citronella, eucalyptus, *clove,* or *atlas cedarwood* spray for an insect repellent or parasites.

Insect Bites:

Put lavender straight (neat) on area.

At the Gym:

Sweet! Sweat: make a spray or lotion with lemon, bergamot, lavender, *thyme, juniper,* or cypress.

Promote sweat, detoxification: Make a spray or lotion with *rosemary, thyme,* roman chamomile.

Played Too Hard:

Swelling, inflammation: Use massage oil with cypress and/or lemon.

Muscle stiffness: Use massage oil with *black pepper, juniper,* and/or *rosemary.*

Stiff neck, shoulders: Use massage oil with marjoram.

Athlete's foot and ringworm: Lavender, tea tree, patchouli.

Overindulgence—Cellulitis, Obesity, Water Retention:

Grapefruit, lime, *fennel,* lemon.

Stale hotel:

Spray with lavender, *peppermint,* and/or lemon to purify and to detoxify.

Caution: *Throughout the text, oils in italics should never be used during pregnancy.*

 Playtime

CHAPTER 6

Assessing Your Life Situation

I've been sharing my consultation stories with you to solidify the concepts of Fragrant Feng Shui through practical application. Each situation describes how a person's life issues are reflected in the layout of their space, and how their furniture and accessories are placed—this is Feng Shui. I hope you have seen reflections of yourself in the stories. As humans, our archetypal needs are the same: We all want to give and receive love—again, the most beautiful of Kabbalistic tenets—to release the fears that hold us back, and to be happy. My problems are the same as yours, as I share my heart and vulnerability with you in my own stories.

We are all connected on the universal level.

In this knowing, we learn to be empathetic and patient with ourselves and others by walking in each other's moccasins.

I have also been asking you to look inside to determine how you can enhance your personal Chi—which is always the first step in making positive life changes. When you live to your fullest, everyone and everything in the web of life benefits.

Each person has a special role to play in the evolution of the planet. Sometimes it's hard to walk your own path because of the pressures that society places on you to conform. From childhood on, you are conditioned by family, the media, elders, and peers about what to wear, how to speak, what to study, what kind of profession is acceptable (and what is not), what lifestyle is acceptable (and what is not), who you should associate with, and who you should avoid. The list is as endless as the possible choices you can make in your life.

None of this conditioning leads you any closer to discovering who you really are and where you would like to go. It only leads you meekly down the lane with all the other sheep. The problem is that since each person is so different, one path is too narrow to include everyone.

Feng Shui is about breaking out of life's restrictive conditioning.

By making changes in the energetic pattern of your life, you can break out of a restrictive mold and evolve into YOU, not into the person everyone else thinks you are.

The following survey can help you identify areas in your life that you need to change, and areas that are doing well but could be improved upon with Fragrant Feng Shui. The questions are based on the body, mind, and spirit issues that we have explored with the Tree of Life, the Chakra system, and the Bagua. As we have seen, these systems are linked through their sacred geometry and representative Chi energies, so it is quite simple to deal with these issues in segments based on the Feng Shui Bagua.

This survey is for your eyes only, so don't fudge on the answers. Respond to the questions truthfully based on your life at this moment. If you haven't done the goal-setting exercise in chapter 2 yet (page 20), please go do it now. It will help reveal how well you know yourself and how developed your personal Chi is.

I would be happy to have you lend this book to a friend, or even better, give one as a gift so you can keep this copy for yourself! However, feel free to make a photocopy of this survey so you can keep it private. Use the following scoring system.

The Survey

+2	if the statement is *a lot* like you/your life situation
+1	if the statement is *somewhat* like you/your life situation
0	if the statement is *neutral*
-1	if the statement is *not much* like you/your life situation
-2	if the statement is *nothing* like you/your life situation

Section 1

_____ You spend several hours a week in quiet contemplation or meditation.

_____ You follow your gut instincts regardless of the consequences.

_____ You have a hobby that lets your mind rest and your hands work.

_____ You are aware of synchronicity in your life.

_____ Your job reflects your spiritual convictions.

_____ You have experienced some type of extrasensory perception: heard advice from an unknown source, seen future events, had a hunch, etc.

_____ Your eyesight is good.

_____ You feel a strong connection to Nature.

_____ You volunteer time to help those less fortunate than you.

_____ You recycle.

_____ You read about or study new topics of interest to you with regularity.

_____ You rarely have headaches.

_____ You have a personal spirituality that helps you lead a better life. This means anything from organized religion to metaphysical groups to your own brand of spirituality.

_____ You pray, give thanks, or do a loving deed daily.

_____ Being silent in the company of others is not uncomfortable for you.

_____ You remember your dreams.

_____ You have finished your schooling.

_____ You are open to others' religious viewpoints even if they conflict with yours.

_____ You take at least one long vacation a year.

_____ You rarely have nightmares.
_____ You do not have any learning disabilities.
_____ Death doesn't frighten you.
_____ You deeply believe that your loved ones who have passed are in a better place.
_____ You accept success into your life.
_____ You feel comfortable sharing your spiritual views with those who ask.

Score _____

Section 2

_____ *Abundant* is a descriptive word for your life.
_____ You have enough money so you don't have to worry about meeting your monthly bills.
_____ You are rarely constipated or have diarrhea.
_____ You trust that with work, you will always have what you need to live.
_____ You have strong friendships with people of diverse backgrounds.
_____ You have a comfortable home in a safe neighborhood.
_____ You splurge occasionally to get something that you really want.
_____ You do not have a weight problem.
_____ You contribute to charities with your money and/or time.
_____ You feel confident and happy.
_____ You rarely have lower back pains.
_____ You take responsibility for your decisions even if they don't turn out as you wish.
_____ You receive joy from giving gifts at unexpected times of the year.
_____ You are not in serious debt.
_____ You do not suffer from liver or digestive problems.
_____ You know you are good, intelligent, and capable.
_____ You say no when you mean it, even when it may make a situation uncomfortable.
_____ You do not have large credit card bills.
_____ You follow your gut instincts.

_____ You live within your economic means.

_____ You participate in causes (environmental, social, political, etc.) that have meaning to you.

_____ You leave any situation that is abusive to you or others.

_____ You enjoy taking long walks or engaging in other forms of healthy exercise.

_____ You would not call yourself a workaholic.

_____ You laugh easily.

Score _____

Section 3

_____ You speak freely with others about how you feel.

_____ You are comfortable with public displays of affection (yours or others).

_____ You are in a healthy, romantic partnership.

_____ You do not mind spending time alone.

_____ Intimacy is an important part of your dating/marriage life.

_____ You say no when you feel like it.

_____ You feel comfortable viewing yourself naked.

_____ You take pleasure in fine food, drink, and good company.

_____ You are comfortable with *your* sexuality.

_____ You do not suffer from impotency or frigidity.

_____ You would give your love life a thumbs up.

_____ You don't use sex to manipulate (i.e., withholding sex to punish a spouse for what he/she did/didn't do.)

_____ You let your emotions out; for example, if you're angry, you let it out in a constructive manner.

_____ You dance, jog, walk, practice Tai Chi, or just generally move with the flow.

_____ You do not have urinary, bladder, or sex organ problems.

_____ Your sex life is unfolding as *you* wish (you are sexually active by choice or celibate by choice).

_____ You leave, or stay out of abusive relationships.

_____ You have good friends who you can confide in.

_____ Your business relationships are strong.

_____ You do not overindulge in food, alcohol, sex, shopping, etc.
_____ You are social and make friends easily.
_____ You are able to express your feelings with others openly and often.
_____ You only have sex to connect with and love another person.
_____ You get joy out of dating (or marriage).
_____ You tell your friends how much their friendship means to you.

Score _____

Section 4

_____ You have a healthy relationship with your parents.
_____ You stay in touch with your siblings.
_____ You have strong ties with friends who are like family to you.
_____ You do not have heart problems.
_____ You do community work.
_____ You have been able to forgive what has happened in the past.
_____ You visit or communicate with your extended family: aunts, uncles, cousins, nieces, nephews.
_____ You feel compassion.
_____ You do not fear abandonment or rejection.
_____ You tell your family how much you love them.
_____ You rarely have upper back or shoulder pain.
_____ You participate in or support world peace organizations, relief groups, human rights organizations, etc.
_____ You truly love your neighbor as yourself.
_____ You are able to let go.
_____ You do not smoke.
_____ You take time to phone, or write a note to, those you love.
_____ You are not possessive.
_____ You tell your friends how much you love them.
_____ You are not afraid of being hurt.
_____ You do not suffer from high blood pressure.
_____ You trust those people who are close to you.
_____ You laugh easily with your family and friends.
_____ Family gatherings are fun for you.

_____ You forgive those who have harmed you in some way.
_____ You forgive yourself when you have made a mistake.

Score _____

Section 5

_____ You know who you are and your purpose on Earth.
_____ You are known for something that is unique to you (your style
      of dress, your laugh, your artwork, your cooking, your job, etc.).
_____ You have frequent episodes of uncontrollable happiness.
_____ You know that the answers to all your questions are inside you.
_____ You are rarely depressed.
_____ Small (or large!) miracles take place in your life; you
      acknowledge and show gratitude for them.
_____ You are able to consciously create.
_____ You are able to travel astrally.
_____ You don't have a nervous disorder.
_____ Your relationships are balanced and harmonious.
_____ You are living the kind of life you have always envisioned.
_____ You make donations anonymously.
_____ You can heal yourself and others.
_____ You don't suffer from migraines.
_____ You have experienced yourself as part of a larger whole.
_____ You make prudent decisions instantly.
_____ You feel connected with Nature and the vast universe.
_____ Boredom doesn't exist for you.
_____ The word *hate* doesn't exist in your vocabulary.
_____ You are comfortable with psychic phenomena that happen to you.
_____ You are aware of your personal power.
_____ You understand grace.
_____ Spirituality is not a separate section in your life, it is your life.
_____ You have experienced connection with God (the Divine
      Essence, Mother Goddess, etc.)
_____ You give service selflessly.

Score _____

115

Section 6

_____   You are able to express yourself freely.
_____   You have a good support system in your life.
_____   Your partner makes your life easier.
_____   You don't often get coughs or colds.
_____   You never lie.
_____   You know when to be silent.
_____   You tell people how you feel about them or situations you are in.
_____   You are a good speaker.
_____   You are centered.
_____   You don't have a problem with people keeping their obligations.
_____   You are comfortable speaking in public.
_____   You rarely have a stiff neck.
_____   You speak out against social and political injustice.
_____   You are a good listener.
_____   Your voice is modulated and soothing to others.
_____   You never criticize others.
_____   You speak what you feel and know to be true.
_____   You share your knowledge with others.
_____   You are surrounded by people who make your life easier and more enjoyable.
_____   Your employees are happy working with you.
_____   You stand your ground when you believe in something.
_____   You don't talk too much.
_____   You speak up for yourself.
_____   There is low turnover in your work staff (cleaning people/baby-sitters, etc.)
_____   You speak _your_ truth.

Score _____

Section 7

____ You truly love your job.
____ You make enough money in your job so you can live a comfortable life.
____ You feel at home in Nature.
____ You do not fear being alone.
____ Your life is stable.
____ You are not a workaholic.
____ You feel grounded.
____ Your life path includes the current career you are in.
____ You do not have bone or knee problems.
____ Fear is not in your vocabulary.
____ You feel energetic.
____ You don't suffer from bulimia or anorexia.
____ You have a healthy trust of others.
____ You do not obsess about money or your possessions.
____ You do not suffer from high blood pressure.
____ You are able to provide for all your life's needs.
____ You are not in a job just for the money.
____ You spend time outdoors.
____ You don't have a problem setting boundaries.
____ Your feet are planted firmly on the ground.
____ Life is interesting.
____ Your job is compatible with your spirituality.
____ You recycle.
____ You volunteer for, or donate to, organizations that protect the environment.
____ You set a good example for others.

Score ____

Section 8

____ Every day is a new creation to you.
____ You love your children (or your friends, siblings, etc.)
____ You are able to be goofy and spontaneous.

117

_____ You sing and dance (even if you are not a "good" singer or dancer)

_____ You create spontaneously.

_____ Your heart feels full of love.

_____ You have a hobby that you pursue.

_____ You take time out of each day to tell your children how much they mean to you.

_____ You coach or mentor children.

_____ You think nothing of getting your hands dirty with some gardening, pottery, a fix-it job, or painting.

_____ You know how to talk with children (not down to them).

_____ You still know how to _play_.

_____ Your children are your most precious gift.

_____ When you are absorbed in a creative act, you find yourself in another world.

_____ You spend some time during the day alone with your creative thoughts.

_____ You use your dreams to help you solve problems.

_____ Your job calls for you to use your creativity.

_____ Your creativity is part of your spirituality.

_____ You share your talents with others.

_____ You are not uncomfortable with children.

_____ You have completed a creative project within the last two months.

_____ You can laugh with abandon.

_____ You know how to be silly.

_____ You are taking a class or are learning how to paint, sculpt, play an instrument, belly dance, etc.

_____ Life is fun.

Score _____

Scoring: Nothing is ever black and white, so a score is just a guideline; it doesn't mean "good" or "bad." If you have a negative score in any of the sections, it would be a good idea to concentrate on these areas first when making Feng Shui adjustments. Scores on the plus side may need some Feng Shui attention to bolster an area, or if the numbers were very high, you might want to take steps to reinforce and enhance these areas.

ℐ ℐ ℐ

Section 1: Self-Cultivation and Knowledge Gua/Third-Eye Chakra
Section 2: Wealth Gua/Will Chakra
Section 3: Marriage and Relationship Gua/Sex Chakra
Section 4: Family Gua/Heart Chakra
Section 5: Fame Gua/Crown Chakra
Section 6: Helpful People and Travel Gua/Throat Chakra
Section 7: Career Gua/Root Chakra
Section 8: Creativity and Children Gua/Heart Chakra

How do your results jibe with the goal-setting exercise that you did in chapter 2? How well do you know yourself and the state of your personal Chi? If there was a discrepancy between the two exercises, spend some more time in your Self-Cultivation area exploring the power of your Third-Eye Chakra. Don't forget to use some Self-Cultivation fragrance (see chapter 7) while you are there.

Divination

The above survey was designed to show you which areas of your life need a vital Chi fix. Here is another way of finding the answers you need: *divination*. This method is as effective as the survey, though perhaps less easily understood by the rational mind.

There are as many systems of divination as there are cultures on the earth. Every ancient civilization had an oracle that they used in order to contact their Divine wisdom. The Greeks had the oracle at Delphi, the Japanese looked to the symbols on the tortoise shell, the Teutons had their runes, while the Chinese threw yarrow sticks and consulted the I Ching. Each culture developed a system of reading energy patterns.

> **Divination works according to natural laws.**
> **It uses an oracle, a system of symbols,**
> **to reflect what is going on inside you.**

Using a divination tool means interpreting what you see represented in the oracle (microcosm) as symbolic of what is happening in your life (macrocosm). So when you use the layout of the runes, or the

I Ching reading, or the pattern of tea leaves in a teacup, that pattern you see in front of you is the pattern that is present inside you. It is really no different from Fragrant Feng Shui, showing you, through how your space and accessories are arranged, what is going on inside of you. And in fact, Feng Shui is itself considered a divination tool!

There is a cyclical connection to this: the state of your personal Chi, whether weak or strong, is manifested in your home, just as your personal Chi is manifested through using a divination tool. And just as the Feng Shui changes that you make in your home improve your personal Chi, the tarot reading (or any other divination tool) will also help you transform your energy.

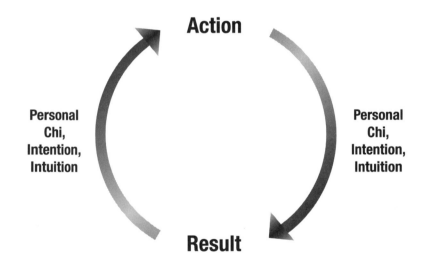

In essence, the action and result wheel is no different from any other natural cycle.[28] The wheel relates to Feng Shui and/or any divination tool, and most certainly to all aspects of the cycle of your life experience. When you use your personal Chi, intention, and intuition to influence you, the *result* then enhances your personal Chi, intention, and intuition. Your newly enhanced personal Chi will provide clarity to determine what *action* is required, and to determine intuitive solutions. The simple awareness that your action flows from enhanced vision will

---

[28] Please refer to *Feng Shui Today: Earth Design the Added Dimension* for an understanding of how Feng Shui evolved and continues to evolve according to the natural laws and all the cycles of nature.

perpetuate your personal Chi and further strengthen your ability to manifest even greater results.

For example, with your personal Chi continually evolving, it becomes ever easier to recognize Feng Shui problems in your environment and creatively design solutions. When fixing such problems, your more highly developed personal Chi will aid in prompt manifestation. These almost magically quick results will further enhance your confidence in your *knowing* ability, so that as your life changes, you can easily recognize the necessary actions.

With respect to life's relationship problems or business situations, personal Chi and intuition quickly help you recognize the required action; also, you receive insight for the right solutions. With each positive result, you learn to trust yourself more, without exhaustive decision making: Intuitive awareness is perceived promptly, and so the actions suggested by your enhanced intuitive abilities can be taken.

With divination tools, your intention to receive guidance must be clear, and your question must be simple and direct; in this way, your subconscious will know which cards, stones, combination of coins, etc., will give you the most insight. By trusting that it was your personal Chi that directed the guidance, you can intuitively interpret your reading, and you'll have confidence and trust in the action that you take.

Perhaps you would like to spritz your favorite Third-Eye and Self-Cultivation essential oil on your body and in the room to get you into the "divination mood."

When you are consulting an oracle, you are simply consulting your own inner wisdom that reveals itself through the symbols of the divination system you choose to use. It is not by chance that certain tarot cards, for example, are revealed. Your energy at a specific moment in time gets manifested through the layout of the cards. If you approach the oracle with an open mind and in a quiet heart place, it will give you a clear picture of what is going on inside you.

Divination tools tap into your essence.
If you remove your attachment to "self," clarity is always there.

The Tarot

This deck of 78 cards is a set of pictures and symbols that represent the full range of human experience. The tarot cards are not playing cards, even though they are said to be the forerunners of our 52-card deck. It is believed that they were designed during times of religious persecution to hold esoteric secrets within their symbols. These "playing cards" were then used as a secret tool to educate novices in universal inner mysteries.

I started playing with them about 18 months ago, and they have since become my favorite divination tool. I consistently, regardless of the question or situation, pick the perfect cards. My personal Chi has grown using them, as every layout I select provides guidance or suggests that I look at my situation in a different way.

I find the tarot a perfect oracle because the symbols on the cards provide insight into the archetypes of man's energetics within universal possibilities. (And, after all, a picture is worth a thousand words.) From "sage-old" tradition, they define the workings of the universe, just as the Bagua and the Chakras do. The Thoth tarot deck, which I prefer, is also intimately linked with the Kabbalistic tradition,[29] definitely a plus for use with Fragrant Feng Shui.

You can use the tarot cards to help you understand your path even if you have never used them before. There is no prerequisite other than an open mind and the desire to look inside. Psychics and mediums who use the cards have practiced using this tool and are able to quickly access that universal intelligence that lives inside each person. With practice, you can do the same. So get a set of cards (or any other divination tool that appeals to you) and a good guidebook and get started.[30]

---

[29] Kabbalistic tradition, as well as the Thoth deck, also includes many universal systems for understanding the workings of the cosmos: astrology, numerology, energetic representations of the 22 characters of the Hebrew alphabet (which also correspond to the 22 trump cards), and so much more. I love it!

[30] Guidebooks do just that—guide. It's like having a good teacher. Once you become good at the basics, give the book away, as no one will be able to intuitively understand your cards better than you do.

T a r o t　　S p r e a d
What Chakra/Bagua Essential Oil will enhance all aspects of my life?

Intuitive Perception / Heart Center / Physical Action		
#7 Crown/Fame Recognition/Attainment	Resolution Card:
#6 Third-Eye/Self-Cultivation Knowing/Spirituality	Deeper Understanding Card:
#5 Throat/Helpful People Communication/Associates	My Question for Clarity is: Card:
#4 Heart/Health Center/Family/Creativity	The Key Card:
#3 Will/Wealth Abundance/Inner Power	Outwardly Seen Card:
#2 Sex/Marriage Relationship/Partnership	Receptive to/Attracting? Card:
#1 Root/Career Journey/Life Passage	"What's Going On?" Card:

Intuitive Perception (sections #5–#7)
Heart Center (section #4)
Physical Action (sections #1–#3)

I need to work with my _____ Chakra/Gua.
Remember to start with your Root/Career card and work your way up from bottom of chart.

The Chakra Spread

You can use the following exercise to explore the Chi moving through your vessels—your body and your home. It can help you understand your issues just as the survey did.

I developed a chart to guide you through a tarot reading. It will allow you to open up so you can be guided by your higher self. In the left column, the Chakra/Bagua energies are listed along with a few key words. The right column gives you the focus of the card you will be choosing to better understand how the energy in the left column is manifesting in your life. The right column has blank space so you can jot down the meaning of the cards, how they relate to your Chakra/Bagua, and any intuitive impressions you receive. All these will help you determine which area of the Bagua/Chakras you want to work with and how to combine your oils.

Exercise:

To begin, find a quiet place where you won't be disturbed. Bring a pen and the chart so you can make notes if you choose. (Feel free to make a copy.) In this sacred space, you may want to have a work surface with a special cloth used only for this purpose. Lighting candles and using fragrant essential oils or incense is a nice way to put yourself in a relaxed state, but they're not necessary.

Sit in a comfortable position with the cards in front of you. Close your eyes and quiet your mind. Gently let go of all outside thoughts. Let the cares of work and family slip away. (They aren't going anywhere and will be right there when you finish, so forget about them for the next 20 minutes.) Breathe deeply for a couple of minutes, focusing your attention only on inhaling and exhaling fully.

You are going to ask that the cards reveal what is going on with you at this moment based on your Chakras and the Bagua of your home. The question you ask might be something like: "What issues are relevant for me to know about each Chakra and each area of my life based on the Bagua?" or "Higher self, please help me understand the dynamic of what is happening in my life based on the energy of my

Chakras," or "How can I understand the problems I am having based on my life issues?" Remember, the clearer your question, the clearer the answer.

Now, open your eyes and begin shuffling the cards while you mix your energy with them—*all the while remaining focused on your question.* Cut the deck and choose three cards (you can choose off the top of the cut deck or, as I like, you can fan them out and choose them individually), and place them face down. Start with the Root Chakra/Career Gua. Focus on your question and how it may relate to that particular Chakra as you select the card. Then move on to the Sex Chakra/Relationship Gua and the Will Chakra/Wealth Gua. Turn the cards over and contemplate what each has to say. These cards will address the *physical aspect and action* behind the question. The first Chakra will tell you what is going on. The second will clarify what type of energy you are attracting or are receptive to. The third will tell you how others around you are viewing you, in terms of what you are experiencing.

Before you pull the next card, the heart card, remind yourself of what it represents—the energetic connection between the physical and the spiritual. Remember to focus on your question as you pull the heart card to see what it says about the key to your issue.

The three "upper" cards will give you more of a focus on what is perhaps not clear about the cards you have just turned over. Quiet your mind again, and formulate a question for clarity. Write it first on the sheet if that will help you concentrate better. Then pull the next three cards in order: Throat Chakra/Helpful People Gua, Third-Eye Chakra/Self-Cultivation Gua, and Crown Chakra/Fame Gua. These cards will speak to you of the higher spiritual aspect of your question.

If you are new at this, spend some time just absorbing the pictures and intuitively trying to understand what the images are saying to you. You can learn a lot by just being silent and contemplating. Then go to your guidebook if you need any additional clarification on what the card means. You can also look at a sample of a reading I did during one of my monthly, new-moon ceremonies.

Tarot Spread

What Chakra/Bagua Essential Oil
will enhance all aspects of my life?

New Moon!
New Year

Intuitive Perception

#7 Crown/Fame Recognition/Attainment	Resolution Card: *Princess of Swords* *Victory over moods, out of the darkness* *into clarity-all that didn't serve me is* *gone-cut through to clarity and vision, not* *to be* *intimidated, pursue vision with the*
#6 Third-Eye/Self-Cultivation Knowing/Spirituality	Deeper Understanding Card: *Love* *Learn to love myself more then it will* *be easier for others to do so, I am deserv-* *ing, let go of all my judgement on myself-* *throat says it is okay!*
#5 Throat/Helpful People Communication/Associates	My Question for Clarity is: *What do I* *need for Abundance/ Success?* Card: *Ace of Disks* *Inner & outer riches-unification of body &* *soul, material & spiritual-wholeness. I give* *myself up to be open to learn to use my* *wings - all* *I need I already have.*

Heart Center

#4 Heart/Health Center/Family/Creativity	The Key: Card: *Moon* *I am ready to first let go of all that does-* *n't serve me - gone! my heart, health, and* *creativity is open to new dimensions. Stay* *connected to spirit daily.*

Physical Action

#3 Will/Wealth Abundance/Inner Power	Outwardly Seen Card: *Abundance* *Overflowing exchange. I have something* *very valuable to share - I do not need to* *look for people who want to receive my work* *- they will come. I have everything I need to*
#2 Sex/Marriage Relationship/Partnership	Receptive to/Attracting? Card: *Success* *Ready!!! External manifestation. I am ready* *to be seen and appreciated on a world-* *wide basis through inner success and per-* *sonal transformation. I show gratitude for*
#1 Root/Career Journey/Life Passage	"What's Going On?" Card: *Knight of* *Disks* *I am master of health and material abun-* *dance. All is well worth it - in service and* *personal growth. All my powers as capable* *and making the effort, all is rewarded.*

I need to work with my *Third Eye/Self-Cultivation* Chakra/gua.
Remember to start with your Root/Career card and work your way up from bottom of chart.

Keep in mind that when the major arcana cards, the 22 trump cards, appear, they signify that you should pay heightened attention to that Chakra/Bagua area. These cards represent human archetypes, and they are trying to tell you about a major energetic shift to be examined. If you receive a major arcana card, later on you may want to go into that particular Gua, and as you sit in the energy of the space do another reading in order to understand the nuances of what the card is telling you. Look around you. What Feng Shui can you redesign?

When you finish, put your cards away, and let your mind just absorb what you have learned. You have just been given a complete mirror of what is happening energetically with your life. Now you are ready to get yourself into Fragrant Feng Shui action. You have a road map of where you need to go. Inhale the fragrant life beauty. Let's not wait. Let's get going on improving your life!

Good Scents

Oils typically blend well within family groups.

Woodies: *atlas cedarwood*, pine, *cinnamon*, sandalwood
Herbies: *basil, rosemary, clary sage,* geranium, *peppermint*
Citrus: bergamot, lemon, *thyme*
Florals: roman chamomile, rose, jasmine, lavender, neroli, ylang ylang
Resins: benzoin, frankincense
Spicies: ginger, *black pepper, cinnamon, clove,* coriander, *nutmeg*
Fruities: bergamot, *black pepper, clove,* grapefruit, *juniper,* orange
Leafies: *cinnamon,* cypress, eucalyptus, patchouli, *peppermint*
Rooties: ginger, vetiver

Try these combinations:

Atlas cedarwood: sandalwood, rose, *juniper,* cypress, vetiver, patchouli, benzoin
Basil: bergamot, *clary sage,* lime, citronella
Bergamot: lavender, neroli, jasmine, cypress, geranium, lemon, roman chamomile, *juniper,* coriander
Black pepper: frankincense, sandalwood, lavender, *rosemary*
Roman chamomile: bergamot, lavender, *clary sage,* jasmine, geranium, rose, neroli, patchouli, ylang ylang, *atlas cedarwood*, vetiver
Cinnamon: ylang ylang, orange, benzoin
Clary sage: *juniper,* lavender,

Mixers

Good Scents

coriander, cardamom, geranium, sandalwood, *atlas cedarwood,* pine, jasmine, frankincense, bergamot

Cypress: *atlas cedarwood,* pine, lavender, *clary sage,* lemon, cardamom, roman chamomile, *juniper,* benzoin, bergamot, orange, sandalwood

Eucalyptus: *thyme, rosemary,* lavender, pine, *atlas cedarwood,* lemon

Frankincense: sandalwood, pine, vetiver, geranium, lavender, neroli, orange, bergamot, *basil, black pepper, cinnamon*

Geranium: lavender, patchouli, *clove,* rose, neroli, sandalwood, jasmine, *juniper,* bergamot

Ginger: sandalwood, vetiver, patchouli, frankincense, *atlas cedarwood,* coriander, rose, neroli, orange

Grapefruit: lemon, bergamot, *rosemary,* cypress, lavender

Jasmine: rose, sandalwood, *clary sage,* and all citrus oils

Juniper: vetiver, sandalwood, *atlas cedarwood,* cypress, *clary sage,* pine, lavender, *rosemary,* benzoin, geranium

Lavender: citrus and floral oils, *atlas cedarwood, clove, clary sage,* geranium, vetiver, patchouli, and most everything else!

Lemon: lavender, neroli, ylang ylang, rose, sandalwood, roman chamomile, benzoin, geranium, eucalyptus, *juniper*

Orange: roman chamomile, coriander, geranium, benzoin, *clary sage,* jasmine, lavender, rose, ylang ylang, lemon, and other citrus oils

Mixers

Good Scents

Patchouli: vetiver, sandalwood, *atlas cedarwood,* geranium, *clove,* lavender, rose, neroli, bergamot, *clary sage,* and orientals

Peppermint: benzoin, *rosemary,* lavender, lemon, eucalyptus

Pine: *atlas cedarwood, rosemary, juniper,* and other woodies

Rose: jasmine, orange, geranium, bergamot, lavender, *clary sage,* sandalwood, patchouli, benzoin, roman chamomile, *clove*

Rosemary: lavender, citronella, *thyme,* pine, *basil, peppermint, atlas cedarwood, cinnamon,* and other spicies

Sandalwood: rose, *clove,* lavender, *black pepper,* bergamot, geranium, benzoin, vetiver, patchouli, jasmine

Thyme: bergamot, lemon, *rosemary,* lavender, pine

Vetiver: sandalwood, rose, jasmine, patchouli, lavender, *clary sage,* ylang ylang

Ylang ylang: jasmine, vetiver, bergamot, rose, and florals/spicies

Caution: *Throughout the text, oils in italics should never be used during pregnancy.*

Allow your oils to evolve for at least 24 hours before experiencing the full fragrance.

Try other blends, too!
Create your own. Have fun!

Mixers

CHAPTER 7

Spritz Away!

Now you can get into fragrant action! It's time to put all your knowledge to work to make your Feng Shui experience and your life better. Have you been spritzing around with one of your favorite scents in anticipation? Once you begin using essential oils, there is no going back to the old, less fragrant way of living.

Fragrant Feng Shui relates to how you can change your personal Chi by using fragrance to help you modify the Chi in your home and body. The areas of the Bagua as well as the Chakras have specific energies. And as we discovered, each plant has a specific vibratory rate. So when you spray the essential oil of a plant into a room or on your body, you are adjusting its vibrational rate, making it more balanced and harmonious. The essential oils that you will be using are designed to balance specific areas of the Bagua and corresponding Chakras. Once you are comfortable using the essential oils in this way, we will move into how to code your Feng Shui adjustments for added benefit. But first, let's get to the fragrant fun! Below are the oils that correspond to the Bagua and the Chakras.

Now that you have done your analysis, survey, and/or the Chakra tarot card spread, you can choose the appropriate oil or oils from the chart and begin to work on balancing your body and your home.

Remember that when essential oils are sprayed or diffused into a

OIL CHART

The Body	Chakra	key words Chakra & Bagua	Bagua Area	Tree of Life	Middle Pillar of Tree	Fragrances
top of head pineal gland	crown	attainment / completion spiritual: awareness / calmness connection / empowered	fame	Kether	crown	roman chamomile, frankincense, jasmine, sandalwood, *clary sage*
brow pituitary hypothalamus	**third eye**	intuition / awakening inner vision /self-cultivation consciousness	**knowledge**	Hod	**knowledge**	lemon, juniper, peppermint, eucalyptus, *rosemary, basil*
throat neck / ears thyroid	**throat**	communication release judgment / service breath of life in assistance	**helpful ones**	Netzach		lemon, peppermint, myrtle, pine, lavender, lime, geranium, *thyme*
heart / breath thymus	**heart**	love to family / children of mankind w/ your center tai chi / heart of home / beauty harmony / comfort / balance	**health**	Tipareth	**beauty**	roman chamomile, lavender, orange, ylang ylang, sandalwood, rose, *clove*
solar plexus pancreas adrenals	**will**	power / energy / centered wealth of personal capacity confidence / courage	**wealth**	Binah		ginger, bergamot, cypress, frankincense, *atlas cedarwood*
lower abdomen genitals ovaries / testes	**sex**	socialization / emotion partnership / relationships pleasure / intimacy	**marriage**	Chokmak		geranium, grapefruit, ylang ylang, sandalwood, orange
base of spine	**root**	security / foundation grounding / individuality journey / life experience	**career**	Yesod	**foundation**	vetiver, ginger, patchouli, *black pepper, cinnamon*

Warning! Pure essential oils should never be applied directly to the skin. Always blend them into a carrier oil or purified water, etc.
Oils in *bold italics* should never be used during pregnancy.

132

room, they have a Chi-altering effect. They change the *note* of the atmosphere, making it more calming, stimulating, and/or reenergized—depending on the characteristics of the specific oil used. Additionally, the aromatic oils add negative ions (which are beneficial) to the air; this shifts the frequency of the atmosphere that has become overloaded with positive ions released by electrical devices.

If there are several Chakras or areas of the Bagua that you would like to work on, you can use a number of oils at the same time. Clearly, some scents work in combination better than others, but don't let that stop you from experimenting. Essential oils are fragrant and fun—how can you make a mistake in choosing a scent?

> **Select an oil that smells good to you.**
> **That is the one that will do you the greatest good.**
> **Your nose knows!**

There are many more essential oils that can be used based on how they influence the body, mind, and spirit; I have selected these, as they are relatively inexpensive and accessible. Rose, for example, is a wonderful oil to use with the Crown Chakra, but at $134 an ounce (versus the $10–$20 per ounce for the oils I have chosen) it is perhaps a special treat more than a spray-it-every-day fragrance. I also encourage you to try oils not included in this list.[31] Trust your intuition, and it will lead you to the oils that you need at a particular time.

Using the Oils

Spritzing and spraying are not the only ways that you can use the oils. Diffusing, bathing, rubbing, massaging...the methods are endless. The point is not how you use them, but that you *do* use them daily.

Make a spritzer bottle of Fragrant Feng Shui oil and get to work!

---

[31] There are many very good aromatherapy books to help guide you to a larger list of oils. I encourage you to do research with these books and with your nose!

Remember, just add 18 drops[32] of your chosen essential oil into a two-ounce, dark glass spray bottle, fill it with purified water, cap it, shake, and spray. How much easier can Feng Shui get? You now have made an essential oil spray that you can use on both your body (go ahead and spray that Chakra) and in your home, in the Bagua area that you would like to work on.

Begin with your body. Use the spray that you just made to spritz your Chakra, or spray your entire body to recharge your aura. You can also make your own perfumed oil to rub on your body. Add 9–18 drops of your chosen essential oil(s) to a 1-ounce bottle of carrier oil such as sweet almond oil, jojoba oil, or grapeseed oil.[33] Mix them together well, and you have a great way to keep the scent with you and on you all day long.

Don't forget to carry your fragrant spray bottle or perfume with you so you can recharge yourself during the day.

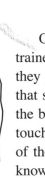

Remember! The oils must always be diluted in purified water or in a carrier oil![34]

Only professional aromatherapists have been trained to use essential oils undiluted. Remember, they pack a powerful Chi punch. There are some oils that should never be used because of their effects on the body. Just as some plants are poisonous to eat or touch, the same is true with their essential oils. None of the oils that are mentioned in this book have any known harmful effects. Care must be used with children and the elderly, as their constitutions are unique. Pregnant women should also be cautious, as some essential oils have abortive properties. A good rule of thumb: If you are not sure about the effect of an essential oil, get advice from a professional aromatherapist.

---

[32] In the Appendix, there is a "drop" chart to assist in your scentual experimentation.

[33] These can be found in any health food store, and should be organic if possible. Non-organic oils can be treated and filtered with chemicals.

[34] This is not just idle advice. Just yesterday, in "the mist of alchemical creativity" (I'm so dramatic), I rubbed my face, not knowing I had oil on my hand. It stung for quite a while and crept too close to my eyes. I venture to say that if I came from delicate blonde stock, I would have burned my skin with my carelessness.

In addition to using the spray in your home, you can also diffuse the essential oil in the appropriate area of the Bagua in order to enhance your Feng Shui adjustments. There are various methods of doing this. One of the easiest is using a ceramic essential oil burner. This is actually one of the oldest methods; archaeologists have dug up ceramic aromatherapy burners in Syria from 1300 B.C. that look exactly like those that are being sold today. A candle or an electric lightbulb goes underneath a small ceramic dish that sits on a pedestal. Fill the vessel with water, add a few drops of your oil, light the candle or plug it in, and you're set. Other inexpensive options include a small ceramic ring that you can place on a lightbulb. As the lightbulb heats the ring, the oil you have placed inside is dispersed. If you like to use candles, let them burn for a bit, and place a few drops of the essential oil you have chosen on the melted wax. Be sure to avoid the wick, as the oils are flammable.

REAR of Your Home, Office or Any Room

3	7	2
Abundance Wealth	Fame Recognition	Marriage Relationships
4	4	4
Family Friends	Health Balance	Children Creativity
6	1	5
Self-Cultivation Spirituality	Career Life Path	Helpful People Associates

FRONT of Your Home, Office or Any Room

You can also invest in an electrically powered aromatherapy diffuser. It is a small apparatus that diffuses the essential oil in timed-release cycles. It disperses them by air flow, not heat (which may alter the chemical structure of the oil). Although they usually cost around $100, they are a sound investment for a business environment where burning candles is out of the question.

The Sacred Geometric Link

Although the diagrams showing the use of the oils on our bodies and homes look simple and straightforward, the relationship between the Chakras and Bagua energy centers is deeply symbolic. The overlay of the Chakra system, the Bagua, and the Tree of Life on page 79 showed us how they are interconnected through their universal Chi energetics. We can also see how the principles of sacred geometry are uncovered at every step of our process. The beauty of these principles is that they work on many different levels, some obvious, some hidden.

REAR of Your Home, Office or Any Room

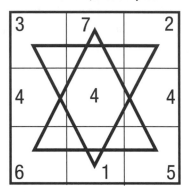

FRONT of Your Home, Office or Any Room

Amazingly, the correspondence of the Chakras when numerically
matched with the Bagua give us a sacred geometric symbol.

When you place the number of the Chakra (one being the Root Chakra/Career Gua, and seven being Crown/Fame) in the corresponding areas of the Bagua, we can again trace a sacred geometric pattern. First, connect one, two, and three; then five, six, and seven. Four, the heart area, is the center.

We have just created the six-pointed star: The Star of David, the Seal of Solomon, and the hermetic symbol of "as above, so below." This is the symbol of balance and harmony: the trinity of the material pointing down, and the trinity of the spiritual pointing up. The triangle/pyramid is also the most architecturally stable of all of Plato's solids.

What a wondrous thing! We are living in a universe guided by sacred rules that govern the harmony and balance in our lives. When we start looking for and using the correspondences that are all around us, we begin living within the fragrant flow of life.

Intention Is the Key

You are still spritzing your fragrances as you read, aren't you? I bet everything is smelling great. In addition, you have been shifting the vibratory rate of both your Chakras and your home, making them more harmonious. Keeping both of your vessels in balance is an important element in making positive changes in your life. When you have vibrant Chi flowing through the energy centers of your body and your home, you are cultivating personal Chi.

> When you have strong, personal Chi,
> you can accomplish anything.
> That, in essence, is Fragrant Feng Shui,
> but it can also be so much more.

You create with your thoughts and perceptions. When you put intention behind your thoughts, you are able to create your future. Feng Shui is about making changes in your life with intention. If you move your furniture or hang a new picture, you certainly enhance your surroundings, but you aren't necessarily making life changes. If you combine intention—thought behind what you want to accomplish—with the movement of furniture or addition of a picture, you actually begin to manifest change. The power of your personal Chi—of your thoughts, your intentions—creates the shift.

How does intention work exactly?

Intent is everything. Without intention, without purpose, you are like a boat drifting down a river. The boat reaches its destination eventually, but not without delays, bumps along the shore, and being carried by strong currents. A life without purpose will follow the same route as this boat. When you use intention and define where you want life to lead you, you are able to manifest everything you need to accomplish your goals.

The same is true with Fragrant Feng Shui. You can arrange and rearrange, spray and spritz, making your house look and smell nice. But without intention behind the decorative changes you are making and the spritzing you are doing, real changes inside you may be long in coming. On the other hand, if you arrange and spritz with the intention of *coding* the specific changes, nothing can stop you from accomplishing them much more quickly.

Thought creates.
Create the kind of life you want to live with clear intention.

Chi Manifestation

What kind of changes do you need to make in order to achieve your dreams? Make sure that those thoughts are clearly in focus when you choose the Feng Shui adjustments you want to make, whether it be moving an accessory or rearranging a room. Keep that visualization centered as you code with focused intent the essential oil you have chosen. And as you spray the oil to link that Feng Shui adjustment to the life change you want to make, maintain that same focus, knowing that the transformation is already in progress. This is the process of creating through your personal power, or "Chi Manifestation."

Although it appears to work magically, Chi manifestation is actually quite scientific. Everything is made of Chi: you, me, the desk, the air, the essential oils, your sofa, everything. Each object's energetic structure shimmers and vibrates in a cosmic dance. They are not solid form; they are energy *bundles* that are simultaneously matter and movement in dynamic relationship. When you intervene in this dance with your creative thoughts, when you *code* it with your *intention*, you shift the Chi of an object. The Chi condenses and recreates the material.

This means that there is no line of demarcation between objects. We are all part of the Divine universal order. And when you are able to access the energetic structure of an object or yourself through your visualization, you are able to mobilize that animating force of Chi to make changes.

Your intention, your personal Chi, influences
the cosmic web to create what you desire.

When I code an area, accessory, or my body with the fragrant intention of my Feng Shui changes, I visualize a computer-generated image:

> *Let's say you want to place an amethyst crystal in the Self-Cultivation area of the room where you meditate, and code it to enhance your connection to Spirit.*

138

In your mind's eye, visualize everything around you as a pixilated image. See your body, the room, the table where you placed the crystal, and the amethyst itself as a series of dots. Everything that is "solid" is now a series of interconnected dots: the amethyst's purple dots, the wooden table's brown dots, your jeans' blue dots...

As you focus on your crystal and speak your intention, your "breath dots" (perhaps seen as bubbles or a film that surrounds your voice, your personal Chi) come out of your mouth and are directed over to the amethyst and settle in between its purple dots. Your Chi is now coded as part of the amethyst.

Additionally, when you speak your intention and spray your favorite Self-Cultivation essence at the same time, the "Chi-enhancing fragrance dots" attach to the crystal and to your body. So every time you experience that fragrance, the scent recharges the cellular memory of your body that has been coded with intention, which in turn is energetically connected to your coded amethyst. Both work together to bring your intention closer and closer to your desired result.

This is literally how the truism, "Thought creates," works. You are able to *see* the change that you want to make, and you *code* the life force of your body, your space, and the accessories to bring that change about. When thought is combined with the essential oil catalyst and then applied to the Feng Shui changes, you begin to shift energy immediately. You already have experienced the power that smells have to bring up memories; now you are merely linking this power of subliminal recall to a future that you have already visualized.

Personal Chi
(your speech/breath)

**Essential oils are the link. Their scent triggers
a reaction that sends your personal Chi spiraling,
manifesting the Feng Shui changes that you desire.**

When you use essential oil on your body and in your home, you are using energies significant to both vessels that will magnify your Feng Shui intentions. Since you have coded the scent in your mind to specific changes in your life, every time you smell it you are magnifying the effect.

All Together Now...

Code your fragrance, body, accessory, or area in your home with your own "computer-generated" image in your mind's eye. Through your own knowledge of your personal Chi, you have identified areas that you would like to work on. Choose one, and use the following method to make those changes.

Code the Fragrance

Learn to be your own alchemist. You can create a spray from those in the chart at the beginning of the chapter, or you can create your own special blend. Creating Fragrant Feng Shui blends can be an ongoing creative process. The ancient perfumers were priests and those in charge of sacred rituals. They understood the power of scent and were adept in using it to magnify the potency of their rites. You can do the same. When you are making your sprays or oil blends, put yourself in a ritualistic mind-set. Make the process of creating your fragrance part of your Feng Shui changes.

Whenever possible, bring the sacred into your everyday life. It infuses your being with life-force energy. What do you think brings more Chi into your life: pouring water and an essential oil in a bottle, or developing a conscious process of choosing the oil through divination and then creating it with intent as to the effect that it is going to have?

**When we put consciousness behind our actions,
our actions become a part of the sacred process.**

When you create your essential oil spray, put yourself in a ceremonial state of mind and add mental imagery to the creation of your blend. Infuse what you are making with your intent. (This can go for *anything* that you create throughout your day!) Code the spray with the positive changes you want in your life. And don't forget to smile and have fun while you're doing it. A little laughter goes a long way in making life enjoyable.

Coding Your Vessels: In a Nutshell

The process of setting your Fragrant Feng Shui in motion is not a long and involved process. There are five easy steps that take only a few minutes to do.

1. Choose your vessel: either your body or home (or office, boat, business...).

2. Spray your chosen essential oil.

3. Visualize your intent.

4. Verbalize your intent.

5. Spray again.

Code Your Body: An Example

I recommend that you set the intent, or code your body, first. Remember, it is your primary vessel and is always with you!

Go where you know that you will not be disturbed for a few minutes. Quiet your mind, fill your heart with the intention of the changes that you would like to manifest in your life, and begin the five steps.

Focus on your Chakra(s), along with the related issue or desire that you would like resolved or enhanced. Close your eyes if you like.

Spray your Chakra(s) with the related fragrance, or your entire body if you like. As you feel the refreshing moisture of the

141

droplets falling on your body, breathe in the healing energy of the essential oils, knowing that they were chosen for your specific intention.

Visualize that your issue is *already resolved* or that your desire *has already happened*. With this image in your mind, linked now with the coded scent of the fragrance, let it penetrate into the Chi of your body, into the depths of your Chakra(s). Let them open them up so they are ready to receive the healing medicinal properties of the oils, and to be enhanced every time you experience the fragrance. The more specific your visualization of the outcome is, the closer you are to the manifestation.

Speak your intention aloud to provide clarity. You may want to spend time *writing your speech down*. When you speak out loud, your specific intention penetrates your entire being; it also sends the vibration of your intention out into the cosmos.

This is an example of what you might say if you are making changes to your Root Chakra and the Career Gua. Use your own creativity to create words and symbols that feel right to you.

> *"With the grounding and stabilizing properties of ginger, all fears about my job and financial security are released, as all my life's needs are always met. I have a solid foundation from which I can trust that my life process unfolds according to Divine Will. And each time I breathe this fragrance, my Chakra(s) opens, and my life expands to its fullness. I release my intention to the universal source, knowing that there is unlimited abundance for everyone's needs to be graciously met."*

You have now begun the transformation. Keep the change fresh in your mind by perfuming your body or Chakra whenever you think of it. Remember to incorporate your special fragrances as part of your beauty/health regime. Make it part of your "inner beauty" routine as well.

If it catches your nose, it alters your Chi!

Once you set the intent, it is done. You do not need to refocus your attention; all you need to do is spritz and code your home!

Code Your Home

Coding your home is the same as coding your body; it is just your other vessel.

Body—Go into the area(s) of your home that your issue/desire relates to. Knowing that you will not be disturbed for a few minutes, quiet your mind and fill your heart. Close your eyes if you like.

Spray the area(s) with the related fragrance. You can also spray accessories specifically placed in this area that are symbolic of your intention. As you experience the refreshing feeling of the moisture droplets falling on your body and filling the room, breathe in the healing energy of the essential oils, knowing that it was chosen for your specific intention.

Visualize that your issue is *already resolved* or your desire has *already happened*. With this image in your mind, linked now with the scent of the fragrance, let it penetrate into the Chi of the area and your symbolic accessory(s) so they can heal you and enhance your experience every time you experience the fragrance. Again, remember that the more specific your visualization of the outcome is, the closer you are to the manifestation.

Speak your intention aloud so your home, specific area(s), accessories, and the universe can hear you. When you speak out loud, your Chi and your specific intention penetrates into your home and being; it also sends the vibration of your intention

143

out into the cosmos. As with your body, you may want to spend time writing your speech down.

This is an example of what you might say if you are making changes to your Heart Chakra and the center of your home (Family/Children/Tai Chi Guas). Use words and symbols that feel right to you.

> *"With the loving properties of lavender, I set the intent and code the heart center of my home so that it generates loving energy to support all other areas and aspects of my life. I also spray the rose-quartz heart (accessory) perfectly positioned in the heart center of the coffee table, in the heart of the room, in the heart of my home to magnify love. As I spray the family area, I am more loving, more compassionate, thoughtful, forgiving, and caring. Relationships with my family and the family of humankind are getting better and better each day. Every time I breathe this fragrance, my life opens fully to receive love, and I am able to be gracious and creative in all my endeavors. I release my intention to the universal source, knowing that its unlimited abundance keeps the hearts of everyone full."*

Whenever you think of it, spray and refresh the air in your home, office, or car. Make it smell good, and give yourself an energetic smell-good charge.

Remember, every time you spritz... if it catches your nose, it alters your Chi!

Code your body and home in tandem to magnify the results: This is the Essence of Fragrant Feng Shui!

While coding your home, code your body at the same time to connect their related energies—the double whammy! Remember, when you speak your intention based on your visualization, speak in reference to your Chakra, Gua, and accessory, if applicable, along with your desire.

Now that your body and your home and fragrance are coded, it doesn't matter where you experience the fragrance; even if you are away from home, the loving energy and intent has already been coded and will support your goals. Every time you spray the fragrance, the Chi you are shifting will be working toward realizing your Fragrant Feng Shui result—even *without* your conscious thought!

⇒Good Scents⇐

Massage:

Good base oils for massage are sweet almond and grapeseed.

Lotions:

For skin oils and lotions, use nourishing oils such as avocado, jojoba, or apricot kernel.

Bath Time:

Euphoric: ylang ylang

Stress, insomnia: roman chamomile, lavender

Aching limbs: *rosemary* and pine

Bedtime:

Spray the room, your body, and bed linens

Aphrodisiacs: *black pepper, clary sage,* cardamom, neroli, jasmine, rose, sandalwood, patchouli, ylang ylang

Sweet dreams: roman chamomile, lavender, rose, frankincense, ylang ylang

Taking Care:

To keep illness from spreading throughout your home and to purify the air: spray, diffuse, and/or humidify with *juniper* and *rosemary*.

To eliminate stale odors (and reduce germs), and keep your home smelling fresh, clean, and healthy: spray, diffuse, vaporize, humidify, and combine biodegradable cleaning products with a lemon, lavender, and *peppermint* blend.

Caution: *Throughout the text, oils in italics should never be used during pregnancy.*

Pampering

CHAPTER 8

Bringing
It All Together

With Feng Shui, you are changing the pattern within your *sur-roundings,* which in turn changes the pattern inside *you.* When you use Fragrant Feng Shui, your home and body begin to mirror the changes that you want to occur on the inside and also act as subliminal guides to keep you moving in that direction. Everything you manifest in your environment comes from the power of your mind to conjure it up, and your personal Chi to set the manifestation in motion.

Manifesting sounds good on paper, but what does it really take to implement such a feat? Sometimes, even though a concept may seem clear, putting it into practice is much more difficult. Let's learn to pick the perfect symbols for your changes, along with just the right position for them within your home.

Using the Elements: The Fun Part!

As a professional interior designer, I love to discuss my favorite things: furniture and accessory selections—the symbols you surround yourself with. The items you choose for your home are critical in man-ifesting Feng Shui results (always combined with setting your intent with good scents). Additionally, your personal design style is a reflection of your personal Chi. When your home is designed to reflect that, it will make you happy. First and foremost:

Do not keep anything in your home that you do not find beautiful, functional, sentimental, or symbolic!

Make sure you don't keep things in your home that are connected to issues that no longer serve you, such as "my mother gave it to me." If you really don't like it but keep it around out of obligation, guilt, or indifference, consider what that says about the relationship you have with the person who gave it to you. Remember that everything is symbolic, so think about the issues that are mirrored in the symbolism of the object. What benefits do you think you may receive as a result of getting rid of the object (donate it to charity!) and releasing the energy held by that object? No mercy, hmm?

Next, when selecting furnishings and/or accessories specific to Feng Shui locations of the Bagua and their symbolic meaning, you might as well integrate the right elemental representation of what you want to accomplish. This is done by incorporating another major Feng Shui concept called the five-element theory.[35]

Remember that the Chinese based their knowledge on the harmony that they perceived in Nature. The five-element theory incorporates these universal natural laws. It uses the symbolism, texture, material, and abstract concepts of the five elements (energetics) of nature—Fire, Water, Metal, Wood, and Earth—to bring balance into living environments. All the questions you might have about using the five elements inside your home can be answered by looking at what Nature does with them on the outside.

You will easily recognize how Mother Nature needs all of the elements to stay in balance. Consider a forest. The trees (the Wood element) need water (the Water element) and minerals (the Metal element), as well as a solid foundation (the Earth element) and the sun (the Fire element) to grow. Feng Shui uses symbolic representations of Nature's creative and regenerative cycles of these elements to make modifications in your home. Using the metaphorical analogies of the

---

[35] Again, I welcome you to read my other two books, *Feng Shui Today,* and *The Feng Shui Anthology,* to learn about this theory and many other Feng Shui theories.

elements, you can incorporate them decoratively into your home, thus making changes in your life. Sound complicated? Nah!

If the elemental representations are obvious to you, just think how intuitive you already are. Perfect Fragrant Feng Shui! Here they are:

Wood:
growth, beginnings,
freshness, nurturing

Water:
flow, clarity,
sensitivity, emotions

Metal:
riches, abundance

Earth:
stability,
grounding, security

Fire:
action,
activity, motivation

If you want to add some energy for new creativity, decoratively add some of the Wood element. If you are bored, add some Fire. Want some sensitivity? Add some Water, and so on. You are only limited by your imagination. Here are some ideas to help you use the five elements.

Wood:

> *design ideas:* furniture, floors
> *color:* green
> *material:* wood
> *shape:* columnar

Water:

> *design ideas:* water features, crystal chandeliers
> *color:* blue
> *material:* water
> *shape:* fluid

Metal:

> *design ideas:* furniture, light fixtures
> *color:* gray, silver, gold, metallics
> *material:* metal
> *shape:* dome-shaped, circular

Earth:

> *design ideas:* stone, ceramic floors
> *color:* yellow, earth tones
> *material:* any earth material
> *shape:* flat, square

Fire:

> *design ideas:* fireplace, carpeting
> *color:* red
> *material:* animal and products made from
>   chemical or heat processing
> *shape:* pointy, angular, pyramidal

Quick Start: On a Budget!

Got 20 bucks? Adding something new to your home brings in new energy. Do you want new: motivation (Fire), joy in experiencing all of life's riches (Metal), opportunity (Wood), stability (Earth), or clarity

(Water)? With cash in hand, go to your favorite modestly priced home-accessory store (Pier One, Bombay, Pottery Barn, etc.), with the intention (you know how to do it now) of purchasing an item that is within your budget.

Budget Ideas

Wood: wooden picture frame or sculpture, plants

Water: crystal/glass/lucite: vases, paperweights, trinkets, mirrors

Metal: picture frames, pretty desk accessories, metallic sculpture

Earth: stone planters, decorative rocks, ceramic vases, or sculptures

Fire: candles, a pyramid-shaped box, picture of a sunset

But Wait—There's More!
(I love this part!)

Consider what issue or desire you would like to manifest, and select your new energy accessory according to which Chakra/Gua it relates to. Have it be the shape, color, and/or material of what you *feel* is the related element for your issue. Once you select your accessory, place it in the Gua that is most representative of your intention. Keep in mind the macro (entire home) and micro (individual room) Baguas. Also remember that these are merely suggestions; only you know your personal taste and what looks and feels good for you.

Example #1: Root/Career

If you are planning to ask for a promotion, you can place an accessory in the entryway of your home, as well as in the Career area of your office. (If you have your own business, you may want to place an accessory in the Career area of your waiting room or lobby as well.) Select an accessory symbolic of grounded, forward movement—perhaps a ceramic or stone statue of a person in motion. The stone is the stable Earth element (you want to be solid in your new position), and the person in movement is you!

Example #2: Sex/Marriage

Want some romance in your life? Let's say the Marriage Gua of your home falls in your kitchen. What can you place there that is symbolic of a good relationship? How about two interlocking rattan heart baskets? The Wood element of the rattan is growth, and the heart shape is symbolic of romance. Additionally, put a romantic accessory in the Marriage area of your bedroom and even in the Marriage area of your nightstand. What about two pink candles? Incorporate the romance of pink with the Fire element of the candles to light up your relationship.

Don't forget to consider all the possible issues for each of the Chakra/Gua relationships. Sex/Marriage is not just romance; it may also include exploring feelings and emotions, your relationship to your higher self, and/or balanced union in a professional partnership.

The following are quick and easy design and accessory ideas for each of the Chakra/Gua areas that incorporate the elements.

Root/Career

Earth: This combination is very earth oriented; you need to have your feet firmly on the ground as you move through your life path. Design ideas: a stone or ceramic sculpture symbolic of your job. On a recent consultation, a stockbroker had a stylized ceramic bull (get it—bull market!) with a very successful attitude on his face.

Wood: Plants, rooted in the earth, are a great addition to this area. When you place a Wood element here, set the intent of growing stability, finances, and new opportunity.

Metal: The Earth generates minerals or metal, so add a metal accessory for abundant joy in your life experience. Accessory ideas: Place your plant from the wood example in a big brass pot.

Water: A mirror or glass accessory in this area could help you see your life's path with depth and clarity. It is also a good addition if your job is stressful (quench a little of that Fire). Be very specific in setting the intent, though, so that your Water element doesn't just lead you to "go with the flow." I personally like to actively participate in life's choices and forge my own path.

Fire: You have to be very careful with the Fire element. Fire is great as a quick charge but should be removed or relocated after the motivating and stimulating energy is received. When Fire is used in excess, it can burn up the energy of the Chakra/Gua, and cause you to burn out. It smothers existing oxygen and may do the same for you. Fire energy is also volatile and unstable. Be careful. Get your charge, then move your intent-full Fire accessory to another area that you want charged!

Sex/Marriage

Earth: If your relationship to your significant other and/or business partner is volatile, Earth is the right element. Design ideas: a heart-shaped rock or a ceramic heart-shaped box. Notice how you can combine the energy of another Chakra/Gua, element, or color for enhancement. Consider the colors of your heart center: pink and/or green. The ceramic piece may have leaves and flowers (Wood) to help the relationship grow and become grounded.

Remember to set the intent <u>with fragrance</u> for all the symbols:

> *"I set the intent, with this pink heart-shaped ceramic box paint-ed with ivy, that my marriage becomes more stable and that it con-tinues to grow from the heart. And as I code my relationship box, may it hold this beautiful energy with grapefruit fragrance. Each time I smell that beautiful scent, all aspects of my stable, loving, and growing relationship are enhanced."*

Wood: Nurture your relationships. What if your heart-shaped box is wooden? Or how about two love birds carved in wood?

Water: Do you want to add clarity and emotional sensitivity to your relationship? What if your heart-shaped box is crystal or glass? Remember to combine the elements for further enhance-ment. Try a pair of crystal candlesticks (Water) with green (Wood) candles (Fire) to grow in clarity, emotional sensitivity, and passion with your partner.

Metal: Metal represents full partnership and abundant love. Design ideas: Try a "romantic" metal sculpture; a pair of metal candleholders with blue (Water) candles for abundant, clear communication and sensitivity; your wedding picture placed in a gilt frame; or fill a champagne bucket with delicate white and pink flowers—fresh or silk.

Are you getting the idea? Be creative!

Fire: Careful again, but...it would be great fun to put red sheets on your bed to add a little passion there. But please take them off after the spark reignites.

Will/Wealth

Earth: Stable finances. Be careful with your intent, as there is a fine line between stable and stagnant. Design ideas: Ground your wealth with a stone pedestal for your wealthy metallic sculpture.

Wood: Let's grow your will and wealth. Consider a healthy plant, or how about a wooden box shaped like a treasure chest left empty, just waiting to be filled with riches...

Water: In traditional Feng Shui, water represents money. How about a tabletop fountain in the wealth area that will keep the money flowing?

Metal: Easy! Select anything metallic: gold and silver picture frames, a dish full of coins from around the world, a metal sculpture, or your heirloom tea service.

Fire: Generate some Fire in your belly and a spark in your bank account. Get a tabletop pyramid that opens (pyramids concentrate and magnify energy), and place the highest denomination bill you can afford inside it. Don't forget the intent of why you are placing it there.

Heart/Family and Children

Earth: For a stable home life, place smooth rocks in this area that have words chiseled in them, such as *peace, love, kindness* (they are available in gift stores — I was given a "magic stone").

Wood: To nurture a strong relationship with your children, frame your family picture in wood.

Water: Clear communication is a must. Set a crystal vase in this area with one flower for each member of the family. Keep the flowers fresh; wilted or dead flowers are Chi-less.

Metal: Place a metal bowl here to represent receptivity to each others' riches and way of being.

Fire: How about a family of different-colored votive candles (again, one for each person in the family) grouped together?

Throat/Helpful People

Earth: Place your collection of ceramic figurines together as your symbolic group of helpful people.

Wood: Group a small "band" of plants in this Gua, representing all your helpful people. I don't recommend cacti because they are thorny.

Water: Clear and truthful communication is crucial in this area. Add a prominent water element such as a fountain or a sizable mirror here.

Metal: Why not make that fountain metal? Or frame that mirror in gold leaf for a wealth of truthful, helpful people?

Fire: If this area is your living room, for example, use a number of throw pillows that incorporate red or angular motifs.

Third Eye/Self-Cultivation

Earth: Get your crystals and other special rocks out into view here.

Wood: If this area is quiet, place a small wooden table here to make a private altar.

Water: Hang a picture of a peaceful and meditative water scene.

Metal: Place your runes or angel cards in a metal bowl where they are more accessible for you to use every day.

Fire: This is a fantastic place for your fragrant candles and incense for en-*light*-enment.

Crown/Fame

Earth: Hang a faceted crystal in the window so it can reflect the sun's brilliance (and yours) into this area.

Wood: Frame a great-looking, recent picture of yourself in wood.

Water: Set a beautiful, cut crystal bowl in this area, leave it empty, and set the intent that it is there to receive the wonders the universe has to offer.

Metal: Why not get a metal wind chime that "plays your tune" to the world?

Fire: This is the element traditionally linked with this area, so get out your candles, pyramids, and red accessories, and live it up with the Fire energy.

Before you start adding and rearranging, keep in mind the steps for Fragrant Feng Shui:

- Assess your life situation/issue/desire using personal Chi and Feng Shui analysis.
- Determine the related energy centers and corresponding essential oils.
- Fix the Feng Shui by "cleaning house," as well as furniture and accessory placement.

- Set the intent, and code your energy centers: "Speak and spray."

- Play with good scents and inhale the results.

Keep in mind all the possibile ways that the energies of each Chakra/Gua can be applied to your life.

Remember to spray and sniff while placing objects, and always set the intent!

Use the Power of Mindful Fragrance!

You don't have to spend money to get started with your Feng Shui changes. Go on a treasure hunt around your house. You will be surprised to see how many elemental accessories you have that merely need to be intentfully placed in the appropriate area.

Select an item that you love, in the element of the new energy you would like to bring into your life. Let's say you've been job-hopping for a while and would like professional stability and job security. The neat-looking rock (Earth) you found (that didn't even cost anything!) on your last vacation would be perfect to place on your desk. (You can't put it in the career area, can you? The rock might be "blocking" your way! But it could be put in the career area if placed in your center pencil drawer.) Now, for the double-whammy—add conscious intent.

As you place the rock, say something while engaging your purposeful desire and belief:

> *"With this beautiful rock that holds such wonderful memories, I set the intent that it will provide job stability and stable growth. All papers temporarily placed underneath [might as well make it functional, too] are charged with secure transactions to not only benefit me, but also my associates, the company, and our clients." [Always include good intentions for all those involved.]*

And for the triple whammy, set the intent with fragrance:

> *"As I spray my stabilizing rock and my office with vetiver, both are coded with perpetuating Root/Career energy. And every time I inhale the fragrance, my intention is acknowledged whether I think about it or not."*

And for the quadruple whammy:

Keep spraying away to bring your reality closer and closer! And remember that each time you spray, whether you are conscious of the intent or not, your nose knows.

Whether you buy a symbolic item, make one, or use one that you already have, always make sure that it is special to you in some way. Remember to take a minute to use visualization, to speak your affirmation, and spray the specific fragrance you have chosen to set the intent. Using all these in combination will magnify your Feng Shui results. You've heard about the "One-Minute Manager"? Well, this is your *one-minute Feng Shui ceremony.*

Remember that the key to your specific manifestation is choosing a symbolic accessory that catches your eye and alters your Chi,

and

using your symbolic fragrance with its specific healing and energetic properties daily.

When it catches your nose...it also alters your Chi!

Use Them Everywhere: Spritz Away!

Use your scents every day, all the time, everywhere. Once they are linked to a specific desire you have, you can start spraying them anywhere, letting the subliminal process of manifestation work on its own. Just experiment with your oils, and let them work their magic. Connect them to everything you do. If you pay attention and work with your energies and the oils, you will be in a constant process of developing your personal Chi while enjoying the good smells around you. It also allows you to always be subconsciously (or consciously!) aware of moving toward resolving your issues, asking for energetic assistance, or manifesting the changes that you want.

Use them daily and throughout the day!

Here are some variations that work for me:

When in town, I prioritize my day so as not to miss my dance class. When I am working on a lot of projects, I find myself not always 100 percent present in class; my body keeps working, but my head can't remember the steps. Blending my favorites of the #1, #2, and #3 "lower body" oils adds some grounding to my etherically oriented Gemini personality. Here I like to use the essential oils in a carrier oil mixture. It smells good when I first apply it, and as my body heats up in class, I get whiffs of it, which keeps me off my neighbors' feet!

If I am spending the day writing, I will spray my favorites from #5, #6, and #7, the "upper," more spiritual, higher-minded oils. I blend them in a spray bottle with purified water and a few drops of carrier oil and use them on my body after showering. It does double duty: I am moisturizing and creating a protective barrier on my skin, while shifting energy into my throat, third eye, and crown. In the office, I spray the same blend, without the carrier oil, when I need to recharge, or I use the oil blend in my diffuser.

In the evening, it is tub time, one of my favorite pleasures. I want everything to come from the heart, and with my tendency to get so focused on everything else, the heart oils keep me in check. There are a lot of yummy options here. You can work with one or more of the #4 heart oils and put 5–10 drops in the tub. Don't forget that the best part is the fragrant steam, so keep the doors and windows shut while you soak. You can also add your oils to sea salt, which pulls toxins out of your body and relaxes your muscles (after all that dancin'). Oh, yeah, I always add bubbles. Afterwards, I either spray myself or use perfumed oil with heart essential oils to settle into sweet dreams.

There are so many ways you can incorporate fragrance in your life, so add your own methods of using fragrance according to your essential needs and desires.

Experiment—it is fun and easy.
Get creative—use your oils wherever and whenever!

For more ideas on your body:

- Create your own perfume.
- Mix essential oil with a fragrance-free body lotion, and voilà!
- Get your partner to give you a fragrant massage.
- Place a few drops in a steamy pot of water for a facial sauna.
- Add a drop on a handkerchief, and inhale—ahh!
- Make an atomizer of flower water to refresh your face midday.
- Carry a little jar of fragrant smelling salts in your purse or car to whiff before a meeting (will/wealth) or romantic date (you pick!).

How about this option? I use a face cream from a mail-order health-care catalog. Depending on the energy I want to work with, I add 18 drops (multiple of 9, a Feng Shui ceremonial number) to the 8-ounce bottle. It is great even on my oily skin, and I get an energetic good shot. Heart-centered essential oil feels like the right one for me — what do you think is best for you?

All these suggestions give you triple-whammy benefits. You get an instant Feng Shui adjustment (you are altering your Chi with all of these, aren't you?); you get the benefit of real essential oil, not potentially toxic imitation fragrances; and it costs you much less to create it yourself.

Make good scents a part of your life.
It will give you so much pleasure.

Don't forget to keep your home fragrant on a daily basis. For ideas around your home:

- Place a few drops of good scents on your air conditioner/heater filter.

- Add some to your dishwashing liquid. Fragrant suds for such a dull job never hurts, and remember, oils are antibacterial, too.

- Vacuuming becomes semi-tolerable with some essential oil in the bag.

- Place a drop or two in the corner of your bedroom pillow (some oils may stain, so use them where they aren't visible).

- Add a few drops to a cotton ball and place it in your undie drawer.

- Scent your bookmarks.

- Use a "signature" scent on your envelopes.

- Spray a fragrance on your sheets.

And don't forget to make up a bottle of each of the Chakra/Bagua scents, and place them in each area of your home. Then as you enter, you can give a quick spray, adding more of the appropriate energy to the space and to you.

You can probably relate to everything I've mentioned above, so why not make each activity or situation a scentual experience? Consider the price of a commercial air freshener (synthetic and potentially toxic) or fragrant bath salts; now you can make Fragrant Feng Shui and life-enhancing blends for a fraction of the cost. So, go to town. Spray and lube yourself up. Be fragrantly decadent!

Create newness in your life while you and your home smell good! Let yourself go, and be creative. Be your own alchemist, creating the perfect blend for you and your Fragrant Feng Shui goals. Now that you know how to use fragrance in tandem with shifting the energy centers of your body and home, you can live unencumbered by personal issues that no longer serve you. Your personal Chi is freed up from restrictive patterns of the past, so you're now able to create a present and a future where you can reach your highest potential.

Real Life: Personal Chi

Throughout the text, I have told you real-life Feng Shui Chakra/Bagua stories. With every consultation that I do, a client's issues and personal life situations are revealed—not only through the pattern of the Bagua, a traditional Feng Shui tool, but also through the Chakra system, which is not traditional Feng Shui. But we know that all the ancient traditions developed from a single source, so their concepts of universal energy centers and the archetypal energies are compatible. Why not use both traditional Feng Shui Bagua and nontraditional tools to get our lives in balance. Makes perfect *scents*, doesn't it?

None of these stories were isolated events happening to someone else. These situations mirrored different aspects of each one of us. Even though some of these stories illustrated issues at the far end of the spectrum, we can all see bits and pieces of ourselves in each one of them. We are here on planet Earth to learn and experience together. Is it surprising, then, how much we can learn about ourselves through the people who surround us?

While we review each of these situations, see if there is an issue in your life that mirrors it. Put some of your newly acquired knowledge into practice, use your intuitive third eye, and ask yourself what Fragrant Feng Shui solutions you would make to overcome the situation. Keep the following in mind:

1. Consider what change needs to be made and what accessory might be symbolic of that change. *Make sure that it catches your eye, so it can alter Chi.* Select something beautiful and decorative that will work within a practical and functional design scheme, with the appropriate elemental representation. Make the item symbolic for the issue and the area where it will be located.

   My suggestions may be different from yours, which is fine. Remember that there are many solutions based upon applying the concepts through individual intuition, symbolic representation, perception, sensitivity, experience, and design style.

2. Select the related fragrance or blend to use as a spray, body oil, etc., with intention.

3. Think of an affirmation that would be appropriate. You may find it helpful if you write it down.

Root/Career

Remember Janette, the divorced woman with the large house who stopped doing her Feng Shui adjustments when the water heater broke (see page 51)? Well, have *you* ever been crippled with fear? Did you ever know that you needed to take a leap into a new way of living but were too afraid? Or maybe it was fear on a smaller scale. Perhaps there was a promotion available that you passed up because you were unsure that you could handle it and you were afraid of losing the security of your old position. These are all issues related to security and not wanting to change. Both of these concepts are illusions, as there is nothing in life that is certain but change. Being firmly rooted doesn't mean you can't grow to great heights. What would your solution be for Janette in her case?

This is a bit of a trick question, because more important than having Janette add to her house, she needed to let go of a home filled with things that held her in the past—*to let go* of her fears. Her biggest Feng Shui change would be to get rid of whatever didn't have meaning for her—via a garage sale, charity, auction, a huge giveaway—*anything* to move that stagnant Chi. I also told her to open up her windows and let in the sun and fresh air. There is no quicker or more effective Feng Shui boost than fresh air and sunshine, along with a good spritz!

I also suggested that Janette make a significant shift in her house (after unloading *everything* that no longer served her) by purchasing the most dramatic accessory or piece of art she could find that was representative of why she was alive. Remember that money wasn't a problem (the old adage that money can't buy you happiness was certainly true in her case), so she could really go all out when selecting a dramatic painting or sculpture. I told her to put it in the center of the house (the den, where she spent the most time) where it would constantly catch her eye and be a symbolic representation of how much fun she could have when she really started living. Being in the center of her home, her heart area, it would support all the other areas, too. I also suggested that she do something similar in the other two rooms that she used frequently.

The moral you can learn from Janette's story is: Don't let your desire to change get drowned out by your fears. It's about letting go of all the stuff that doesn't serve you, because in doing so, you are also letting go of your fears, which don't serve you either. If you find something in your home that is less than beautiful, get rid of it and start living a better life.

As you clean up the old fears that are crowding your path and choking your roots, you might say the following affirmation:

> *"As I gather up these objects that no longer have meaning for me, I realize that they are now a part of my past that no longer serves the person I am becoming. I am spraying my Root Chakra with ginger so that this strongly rooted plant can give me the strength to stand firm in my new path (new career, new attitude, etc.), and I am spraying it in the Career area to help me clear my mind, heart, and home of the fears that have held me back from reaching my potential. I am also spraying these objects that I am giving away with the firm belief that they will bring joy to those who are to receive them now."*

Sex/Marriage

Move now to the story of Maryann (see page 55), who was unable to break out of the mold that held her in a subservient position to her husband, Steve. The imbalance in their relationship revealed that they were holding on to outdated concepts of marriage, partnership, and the role sex and money play in it all. This was a very complex situation. It involved Maryann's Root/Career area, as she didn't have a firm foundation to stand on. It also involved Will/Wealth issues; Maryann was unable to stand in her own power and speak up for herself. All of these issues then manifested in the Sex/Marriage area as an unbalanced relationship.

Step back and examine *your* situation. Are you participating in a relationship(s) that keeps you in role(s) that you no longer want to play? Are you giving your "unconscious" consent to let these relations continue? Do you use sex as a means to an end? Do you use money to shape a relationship?

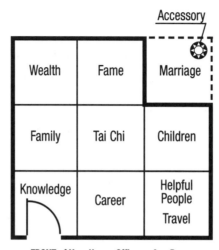

FRONT of Your Home, Office or Any Room

Maryann and Steve's house was L-shaped, so they were physically missing the Marriage area of their house. What could they do on the outside of their home to square this area off so it would be symbolically included in the layout?

How about if in the missing corner they placed a beautiful set of cast-iron garden chairs (remember for relationships you want two-zies) to enrich their relationship? They also could plant a bed of romantic pink flowers.

On the inside, in the room facing the missing area, I would put an electric diffuser with ylang ylang or geranium and have it continually spritz the scent of balanced relationship and romance into that area. Their bedroom would be another area to concentrate on, pairing up symbolic accessories along with adding colors and textures that would enhance their partnership. What do you come up with? Can you think of an appropriate affirmation? How about:

"Ylang ylang, just by its double name, speaks to me of the equality that is now entering my partnership. With each spritz in the Marriage area, we will be drawn closer as we each bring to the relationship the wealth of love and talents that we have to share with each other. I spray my aura with this romantic fragrance so that it may balance not only my Sex Chakra, but all my Chakras as they work together to bring me the joy and happiness I deserve."

Throat/Helpful People

John was the gentleman who would literally rather die than speak his truth (see page 99). Granted, this is an extreme case, but you must ask yourself when in your life you have failed to speak your inner truth. When have you covered up a true feeling or a heartfelt opinion because you were afraid of the consequences? Have you ever not spoken the truth and had it come back to haunt you? Do you surround yourself with loving friends who support the truth that you want to live?

What would your solution be for John and his wife, Judith? I'll warn you that this is a bit of a trick question, too.

First and foremost: **Clean up the clutter!** There was so much junk piled up that had collected dust, it was no wonder John had trouble breathing. Clean, clean, and clean! Purge, purge, and purge! If it no longer serves you or you don't love it, out the door. No mercy! Don't let *things* get in the way of healing—ever. For John and Judith, it was also critical that they clean out their Self-Cultivation area, which had become a dumping ground. (I wasn't able to even walk through the room.) Until they learned to cultivate their inner selves, no healing was going to take place.

The Helpful People room was where John shook off the effects of his chemotherapy. It was dark and dreary. He needed to open up the windows and shades and let the natural light (and people who can help) in! This also symbolizes opening up to the possibility of life, getting the power to start processing the truth. So far we haven't spent a dime, and we've made major Feng Shui adjustments!

John could also hang a picture of an expansive, wide-open landscape picture in the Helpful People room. It would remind him of the wide-open possibilities that life has to offer. Nature is alive and abundant with energy, just as life can be if you say yes to it.

An appropriate affirmation would include "speaking your truth":

> *"With this lemon fragrance, I am bringing the brightness of the sun and truth into my life. As I spray this room, the abundant energy of the universe fills this space. It helps me manifest the abundant help and support that I need to speak my truth to myself and to the world. As I spray my Throat Chakra, I feel it opening to the truth; the lemon is cleansing and revitalizing my throat energy with the power of the spoken word."*

Third Eye/Self-Cultivation

Lisette was dealing with a broken engagement, but in truth, she first needed to understand who she was and what she truly wanted out of life (see page 87). Many people spend their lives fulfilling roles that society has set for them, which have nothing to do with their inner needs and desires. Until you step back and look at who you truly are, you will not be able to manifest the people and things around you that support the true you. You will only continue to manifest based on others' view of who you are.

When was the last time you sat quietly by yourself for an hour just to think about who you truly are on the inside? Do your lifestyle and the people that you have included in your life support that vision? Do you take time out of your busy schedule to read contemplative literature or to meditate? Do you sing or dance to the rhythm that you hear inside your heart?

For Lisette, there were quite a few solutions that she could easily incorporate into her home and life. What would your suggestions be?

Since the Self-Cultivation area of her condo was in her cluttered garage (does it surprise you, based on your knowledge of Feng Shui?), Lisette had to straighten up that mess to compensate for the fact that this area was not inside her livable space. I asked her to establish strong *micro* self-cultivation areas within each individual room's Bagua.

In the living room's Self-Cultivation area, I had her position a comfy chair with a metal lamp (abundance of inner light and vision) beside it. I also had her move her picture of the goddess, Kuan Yin, next to the chair. In this cozy space, she could do her reading or contemplative work. In her bedroom, she liked the idea of setting up a personal altar in the Self-Cultivation area, filled with items that had spiritual symbolic meaning for her.

Remember the broken sculpture of the couple? I asked her to go out and buy a sculpture of a woman with an "attitude" of playfulness and independence—if possible, made by the same artist she liked so much. I asked her to put it in her front foyer so that she would be reminded of her new vision of herself every time she walked into her "new journey."

An appropriate affirmation would be:

> *"With* rosemary,* *I spray my third eye to open up my vision, so I may see who I truly am and know my place in the world. As I spray the Self-Cultivation area of my living room, I am incorporating the energy of self into my home. I spray this chair that it may support me in my personal search; and this lamp, that it may light my way; and this picture of Kuan Yin, that she may guide me. In this Self-Cultivation area of my bedroom, I spray this altar, that it may help me reveal the true me that I know lies within. And as I spray this sculpture, I am confident of the new me that is now taking shape."*

Caution: Rosemary *should never be used during pregnancy.*

Crown/Fame

Fran was the psychic who had an imbalance in her Crown/Fame area (see page 92). She was not able to show others her true manifestation: her self and her art. Ask yourself if the world is seeing you as you truly are. Are you manifesting abundance in your life to your fullest potential? Is the person that you feel you are on the inside, the same person that goes to work and socializes with your friends?

Solutions for Fran's dilemma were straightforward. Adhering to the proper use of Feng Shui, the first thing to do is get rid of what doesn't serve you. Fran's distorted mirror came down. In its place I suggested she put up a great piece of "metaphysical art" showing dimension. And since it was her business to be "way out there," it could be a celestial view showing deep space and the dimensionality of her life. It would be symbolic of her sight into inner mysteries and the depths of her resources, as well as into her client's body-mind-spiritual essence. It was a big wall, so I told her to make it a big piece. Fame is about remembering. What better symbol than a memorable piece of dimensional art?

I suggested that Fran get special translucent window treatments, the type that lets natural light in, to cover the view to the pool. In this way, the lighting would still be appropriate, but Fran's (and her client's) vision would not be watered down by the pool outside.

What would your affirmation be like for Fran? How about:

> *"With the visionary smell of frankincense, I spray the Fame area of my home so that it will reflect my universal wholeness and the personal power that I possess. May it also assist my clients in recognizing their own spiritual truths. As I spray this picture (perhaps spraying nearby so as not to damage it), I am confident of my abilities and my power to help myself and others connect with their higher source."*

Did you see yourself in any of the stories?

What are your stories, and what ideas do you have to change your own life?

What objects in your home can you relocate and set the intent for right now?

Will/Wealth

Do you remember my personal "bag-lady" story—where I mentioned that I never wanted to experience what my mom went through with her finances after my stepfather's death (see page 8)? This issue was centered in my Will/Wealth area. It was about overcoming my fear of being destitute (fear is not just a first-Chakra issue; it can come up in them all) and striking a comfortable balance with my personal and financial independence. Do you have similar concerns? Has your fear of not having enough funds to pay the bills overshadowed other aspects of your life? Is money the mitigating factor in your life decisions? Do you use your personal willpower to stand up for yourself? (Remember

Maryann!) Is your life abundantly joyful? What would you do to activate the Will/Wealth area with Feng Shui?

As a solution to my problem, I located my office in the Wealth area of my home (great also for the Root/Career link). On the micro level in the Wealth area of my office, I placed a $2 bill that one of my clients gave me, as well as a metal basket with the red envelopes that I receive payments in. I also added a plant in a metallic pot (grow that wealth!) with a grinning "beanie" frog that constantly reminds me to lighten up and smile. I have spritzed these with the following intent:

> *"As I spritz this* atlas cedarwood,* *its depth and fullness pervades the Wealth area. I am creating an animated cycle of giving and sharing in my life. Abundant loved ones, friends, clients, and employees will fill my office, my home, and my life. As I spray my Will Chakra, I am opening myself to the riches that the universe has to offer, knowing that through my personal power, I will always have my needs graciously met."*

Caution: Atlas cedarwood *should never be used during pregnancy.*

Heart/Family and Children

Remember how I forgot to link my heart to my life, and how I disconnected the spiritual aspects from the physical aspects of myself? Look at your own life to see if you have a similar situation. Is your heart center full? Do all your actions radiate out from there? Do you let your heart integrate and balance your physical needs with your spiritual needs? Do you let your family know how much you love them?

To enhance this issue with Fragrant Feng Shui, I told you how I selected the rose-quartz heart (Earth element to ground the connection) with its symbolism of love, placed it in the center of my home, and spritzed it. What are some ideas that you have for *your* home?

Keep in mind that this Chakra connects *all* the others, as heart always does, so make sure that you are feeding it loving vibrations. Because of the structure of the Chakra system, with heart connecting the physical/action-oriented "lower" Chakras to the intuition/perception-oriented "uppers," it is the center source of all manifestation. I gave you the affirmation that I used with lavender; now create your own, tying in the heart as the central spiral of manifestation in your life.

In telling you my own personal stories, I have chosen to show you my underbelly so you can see that *all* of us are human and have the capacity to improve ourselves and enhance our lives. My Will/Wealth issues stem from long ago, and my Heart/Family issue is something that I just recently recognized. Working so hard to compensate for my Will/Wealth and Root/Career issues, I sometimes leave my heart out, which is not fair to anyone, including myself. It is ironic that what I want to share the most in this lifetime is what I often forget.

As they say, you have to sweep the floor before you can own the company. We all must work toward resolving past Chakra issues, balancing them all, from the root to the crown. Take a look at your *stuff*, including issues that may have been following you since childhood. Acknowledging it to yourself is the first step of transforming and enhancing your personal Chi.

Let go of your "stuff," and start living!

This work asks you to be tough and to be in touch with yourself, which is sometimes difficult and painful. But once issues are recognized, the healing begins, and Fragrant Feng Shui can make the resolution much easier. It works! The alchemy—your alchemy—can be magical!

Keep in mind that Feng Shui is not just about the heavy-hitting issues. The path to greater health, wealth, and happiness is paved by first resolving your issues, big or small, and then by cultivating your personal Chi. Your holes must be filled first. Then, when you have a sturdy, leak-free vessel, you will be ready to receive and retain everything good that the cosmos has to offer.

Remember: Everyone walking the planet is a work in progress, on a continuous journey to improvement.

Clearings

We have been concentrating on specific areas of the Bagua in con-
junction with the Chakras. When you balance individual areas that need
help, you start manifesting your true desires. There are also ceremonial clearings that you can do to enhance the Feng Shui of your entire
home at once. These are especially helpful when you are going through
some kind of turning point in your life and you need the support of all
your Guas and Chakras to fortify your personal Chi. They're also beneficial when you're making the energetic shift into your new life phase.

Doing clearings is helpful in many personal, Chi-altering situations, both joyful and sorrowful, such as moving into a new space, the
death of a loved one, an upcoming marriage, the loss of a job, the beginning or ending of a special relationship, the birth of a child, embarking
on a new career, or perhaps just for an overall charge to boost your life.
Any time is a good time for a charge: Consider New Year's, your birth-
day, or today!

Through the Black Sect Tantric Buddhist tradition of Feng Shui, as
taught by Grand Master Lin Yun, I would like to share one of the most
remarkable Feng Shui ceremonies I have used, called *Tracing the Nine
Stars*. Its simplicity and power is profound:

> *My intention was to have guidance for what to do next on my life
> path. In accordance with Nature's perfect order and asking for new
> beginnings, I purposefully did the ceremony on the new moon in
> Aries. As I moved through the Bagua, I expressed gratitude in all the
> areas for previous support that I was given, and asked each, accord-
> ing to its energetic representation, for a vision that was in my best
> interest to serve the planet. Within two weeks, I "knew" that I was
> supposed to pull together my second book,* The Feng Shui Anthology.

You can trace the Nine Stars on the Bagua of your lot, your whole
house, office, or even an individual room or work cubicle. The ceremony traditionally consists of moving through each area of the Bagua
(physically or in your mind's eye) following a specific pattern to activate and balance Chi within your space (and, consequently, your life).

I prefer to literally walk through each area to physically engage my personal Chi with each Gua, and vice versa.

Master Lin always encourages us to go beyond his teachings and our own personal limitations. Following his masterful advice, I have integrated the Chakras and fragrance into this "sage-old" ceremony. Let's get the Chi of all of our energy centers engaged and coded with the living Chi of plants.

Select a time when you will not be disturbed for about 30 minutes. I like to prepare a basket of all seven Chakra/Bagua blends to code my body and home as I move through the nine stars. Sometimes I even place an appropriate accessory or symbol ready to be coded on my path. To begin the ceremony, first you do a quiet meditation to still your mind, heart, and body. You might use a traditional prayer that you know or one you have created.[35] In the quietness of your Highest Self, consider a question, desire, and/or intention that you would like your home and the Universe to answer with support, guidance, and/or comfort.

"I ask in my highest good and for those around me, in sincerest intention and gratitude, that _____."

Holding your intention, begin tracing the path through the nine areas of the Bagua. The order is as follows: Begin with the Family Gua, then move to the Wealth Gua, to the center or Tai Chi, the Helpful People Gua, the Children/Creativity Gua, the Self-Cultivation Gua, the Fame Gua, the Career Gua, and the Marriage Gua. Don't forget to send blessings to all those who have supported you in each area of your life.

While in each Gua, focus and speak out loud your:

- intention (it might be helpful to write one for each Gua before you begin).

- appreciation and thanks to *your* Gua and Chakra for all its love and support in the past, the present, and in the future. Release and clear any Gua and

---

[35] Perhaps you would like to use the Heart Sutra meditation, also from the Black Sect Tantric Buddhist tradition, shared by Ms. Crystal Chu in *The Feng Shui Anthology*.

Chakra energy that does not serve you (old owners, old lovers, or any unwanted emotional or spiritual attachment/energy) as you spray your related fragrance blend.

- intention to have *your* Gua and Chakra continue to support your personal Chi with its specific energies. Reinforce the connection with your Chakra (perhaps you want to massage the acupressure point) and the Gua as you spray them again, coding both. Know that your body will support your intentions with the related Chakra/Gua energy even when you are not at home.

- intention to fragrantly code your symbolic accessory to further hold and support your changes. When leaving each Gua, you may want to spray the path between the Guas with fragrance, clearing and coding the entire space. For example, when leaving the Family area, spray lavender halfway to the Wealth area, then spray *atlas cedarwood** the rest of the way.

*Caution: Atlas cedarwood *should never be used during pregnancy.*

When you finish your visit to the Marriage Gua, I suggest you go back to the center to close with something like:

"With the balanced and open energies of my body and my home, all wonder is available to me. I am supported, loved, and nurtured in all aspects of my life; I am ready to receive the grace of the ever-abundant Universe. I am filled to capacity, as I smell the sweetness and gift of my life."

Follow with the prayer of your choice.

"With all that I am (all my personal Chi), in gratitude and appreciation, I ask that the Universe continue to provide a clear path filled with love. Om Ma Ni Pad Me Hum; I am one with Nature; I am one with the Universe."

This is just a guide for you to develop life-enhancing personal ceremonies. They *do* alter your personal Chi, creating positive life changes. If you are stuck, perhaps you might want to browse in your favorite bookstore's spiritual, self-help, or New Age section. Better yet, go into the Creativity (Children) area of your Self-Cultivation room with a quiet heart and your heart essence, along with a pad of paper and pencil, spray away, tune in to your creativity and Higher Self, and ask for guidance. It *will* flow—try it!

 Do your ceremonies according to the natural Earth cycles. Remember the Chakra/Bagua tarot sample that I shared with you? I did it during the new moon. As I calmed my heart in preparation to focus on my intention, a thought popped into my head that I should spray each specific fragrance (already coded with my personal Chi) while drawing each Chakra/Bagua card. This way I would have greater intuitive clarity to interpret it. Voilà—a ceremony! Another fragrance usage! Try it! Then every time you experience any of the scents, you will consciously be reminded of the new beginnings in the shift that your cards suggest.

Try incorporating scent-ual ceremony with other forms
of divination while doing all your spirit work:
meditation, walking in the woods, loving, playing, and yes,
even when you're working or washing the dishes.

The ancients say, "In life, you chop wood and then you carry water." When you tap into Spirit and become enlightened for that one moment, you still "chop wood and carry water." How long can you hold the grace and magic of that fragrant moment? And when you slip out, as we all do, do you remember to come back home?

Coming Home

Without hesitation, what gives me courage to work on resolving my underlying issues and developing my personal Chi is knowing that my fears are the same as yours. Together, realizing that we are connected by the universal gift of life, all our fears can be eliminated.

Our elders, in all sacred traditions, recognized the universal nature of existence and gave us the language to grow our own Tree of Life, integrated with the energy centers of our bodies and homes. These teachers also knew that human beings needed a connection to the Universal Source. By observing the universal laws, the wise ones linked God, Great Spirit, Creator, and the Universal or Cosmic Energy to a cosmology that our earthbound minds could comprehend. The Tree of Life, the Bagua, and the Chakra system are the symbolic representations of this sacred connection. This is the Spirit of Humankind, and also of Fragrant Feng Shui.

The Spirit of Humankind is not tied to any one view of the cosmos. We are all connected by the unity of our humanness and spirit, regardless of our traditions. At our source is universal wholeness. Spirit teaches that when we are connected to our source, we are complete, safe, and loved within the whole to develop and evolve into better and more spiritual individuals.

The spirit of Feng Shui is not tied to any one tradition either. Instead, it asks only that we manifest to our fullest potential by developing our personal Chi and exploring our spirituality. It is all right that we sometimes forget this in our daily routine. Spirit is magical—the second that we realize we have been out of touch, and most likely, out of sorts, our spiritual connection is right back in place. Using fragrance helps us make that connection on a daily basis. This is why I suggest that everyone work with good scents. It is a gift from the spiritual source, which means that it is a part of our connection to universal wholeness.

Just one spritz holds our connection and subconsciously
liberates our fear of separation.
Fragrance helps us maintain a sacred connection
and opens the gates of potential.

So be aware, keep tabs on your Personal Chi, move accessories around, and change fragrant energies as *you* grow and evolve. At different stages of life, different times of the year, and even different times of the day, shift your intent and energy depending on what you want to accomplish. You can always use Fragrant Feng Shui in your life.

Move an accessory and give yourself a spritz!
Create the life of your essential intention!

The magical by-product of manifesting your Fragrant Feng Shui desire is that you also satisfy your responsibility to Humankind. Receiving and sharing, sharing and receiving—sound familiar? Feng Shui helps you develop your spiritual self as you cultivate personal Chi. And the more evolved you are, the more you are able to give back to Humankind and Planet Earth, as this ancient Chinese proverb says so beautifully:

"A bit of fragrance always clings to the hand
that gives you roses."

And if I may add,

Let us all learn to give our hearts away...
Sharing and Receiving.

Through the *scent*ual ability of your body, mind, and spirit, you can lovingly create the fullness of life that comes with all its fragrances.

Now, just one more thing...Fragrant Feng Shui is easy! Why use Fragrant Feng Shui?

It smells good and will enhance your life...
making it better and better!

178

How do you incorporate Fragrant Feng Shui?

**Code your body and home with intention,
develop your personal Chi,
and SPRITZ!**

When your life is full, you are happy. This feeling is received by those around you, and they in turn spread feelings of balance, joy, and happiness to others on the planet!

Conversion Chart
(approximates)

10 drops	$1/10$ tsp.	$1/96$ oz.	About $1/8$ dram	About $1/2$ ml
12.5 drops	$1/8$ tsp.	$1/48$ oz.	$1/6$ dram	About $5/8$ ml
25 drops	$1/4$ tsp.	$1/24$ oz.	$1/3$ dram	About 1.25 ml
50 drops	$1/2$ tsp.	$1/12$ oz.	$2/3$ dram	About 2.5 ml
100 drops	1 tsp.	$1/6$ oz.	$1 1/3$ dram	About 5 ml
150 drops	$1 1/2$ tsp.	$1/4$ oz.	2 drams	About 7.5 ml
300 drops	3 tsp.	$1/2$ oz.	4 drams	About 15 ml
600 drops	6 tsp.	1 oz.	8 drams	About 30 ml
1,200 drops	12 tsp.	2 oz.	16 drams	About 60 ml
2,000 drops	20 tsp.	3.3 oz.	26 drams	About 100 ml

1% dilution	5–6 drops essential oil per ounce of carrier oil
2% dilution	10–12 drops essential oil per ounce of carrier oil
3% dilution	15–18 drops essential oil per ounce of carrier oil

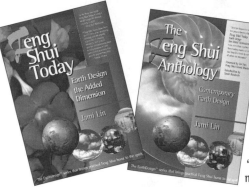

182

About Jami Lin

Jami Lin is an internationally renowned lecturer and consultant on Feng Shui who has authored two Feng Shui books. Forty of the top Feng Shui worldwide experts joined in her visionary project, *The Feng Shui Anthology: Contemporary Earth Design*, which has been called "a Feng Shui masterpiece" and "the standard by which all other Feng Shui books are measured."

Jami's first book, *Feng Shui Today: Earth Design the Added Dimension*, forged new territory in the field of Feng Shui and was heralded as "a breakthrough and an absolute necessity to read."

A graduate of the University of Florida School of Architecture, with over 20 years' experience as a corporate and residential interior designer, Jami has pioneered the transformation of Feng Shui into an approachable tool for mainstream use. Her firm, EarthDesign,™ integrates interior design and self-development, bringing Feng Shui home to the spirit.

In Jami's exciting how-to video, *Feng Shui Today: Enrich Your Life by Design*, noted as "the industry's finest," her expertise in Feng Shui, interior design, and spirituality are combined with the creativity of a multi–Emmy award- winning team. Jami Lin is also a certified aromatherapist with the National Coalition of Certified Aromatherapists and Aromatologist Practitioners and has created the *Feng Shui Essentials: Chakra/Bagua Oil Blends,* which are an excellent complement to *The Essence of Feng Shui*.

Jami welcomes inquiries on seminars and workshops, continuing education programs, consultations, and complete Feng Shui Interior Design (as outlined at the beginning of this book).

Please feel free to contact Jami Lin at:

Earth Design
P.O. Box 530725, Miami Shores, FL 33153
305-756-6426 • 305-751-9995 (fax)
E-mail: earthdes@gate.net
Website: www.gate.net/~earthdes
(regularly updated with new ideas, classes,
and decorative Feng Shui products)

If you would like to receive Jami Lin's favorite Feng Shui tips, please send her a self-addressed stamped envelope (with $.55 postage).

⋞ ⋞ ⋞

We hope you enjoyed this Hay House book.
If you would like to receive a free catalog featuring
additional Hay House books and products, or if
you would like information about the
Hay Foundation, please contact:

Hay House, Inc.
P.O. Box 5100
Carlsbad, CA 92018-5100

(760) 431-7695 or **(800) 654-5126**
(760) 431-6948 (fax) or **(800) 650-5115 (fax)**

Please visit the Hay House Website at: **www.hayhouse.com**

⋞ ⋞ ⋞